JAMES BARBER
IS

the
URBAN
PEASANT

The Urban Peasant Quick & Simple
First Published 1993

By
Urban Ink.

Production Coordination
Romney Grant

Layout & Design
Minds Eye Communications Inc.

Printing
Hemlock Printers Ltd.

Research Assistant
Faustina Gilbey

Illustrations
James

The Quick & Simple Cookbook
was printed on recycled stock.

1st Edition, 5th Printing
ISBN 0-9697123-0-8

Good cookbooks are romances. Food starts off being a private affair between you and your stomach, a simple process of survival and nothing more, but suddenly the taste buds develop, and even if you eat nothing but meat and potatoes you have a preference for meat and potatoes in a certain style, on a certain plate, and maybe with you sitting on a favourite chair.

That's when the cookbook sellers have got you, for life. Like bingo, cigarette smoking, fly fishing or chasing the opposite sex, once is seldom enough. You tiptoe through your first cookbook with all the joy and wonder of a first time traveller in a foreign country (or a kid in Disneyland) and it's not the actual recipes that excite you, but the ideas. Ginger with fish, nutmeg with leeks, grapes with chicken—they're all ideas which make you want to go a little further, see a little more, and try something new.

I like to write romances almost as much as I like to live them, and most of my cookbooks are blatant attempts to seduce, to encourage people to experiment and wander up the sideroads of their imaginations. But this book doesn't need all the sales pitches, it doesn't need the stories of where I found this idea or that, because the Urban Peasant television show has already done that.

So here you are, the first completely practical cookbook I've ever written, no trimmings, no romance, just the basic recipes the way we originally did them on the show. In case you're curious (and from the letters it seems a lot of people are) we do cook honestly on the show, we don't have a second kitchen hidden behind the scenes, and we cook almost everything in real time. If something has to freeze for an hour or spend an hour in the oven we tell you — you don't want to spend all that time looking at the hands of the clock go around. But almost everything you see is cooked with real ingredients, just as you do in your own kitchen, in a hurry and with no fancy tools.

This cookbook is not a romance, it's not about food to freeze, nor to keep waiting on the stove, nor to worry about, it's mostly about supper in a hurry — food you don't have to go very far to shop for. I hope you enjoy it.

CONTENTS

CONTENTS

CONTENTS

CONTENTS

CONTENTS

DESSERTS & DRINKS

CONTENTS

DRINKS

SOUPS

CARROT SOUP

1 carrot - grated
1 onion - coarsely chopped
Ginger - finger length piece, grated
2 Tbsps. butter
2-3 cups water
1 tsp tarragon
1/2 tsp salt
Freshly ground pepper
Yoghurt - small tub
1/2 orange

Heat butter in saucepan and add the grated carrot. Toss in the chopped onion and grated ginger and stir. Pour in 2-3 cups of water, 1/2 tsp salt, some freshly ground pepper and tarragon. Simmer for approximately 10-15 minutes. Squeeze the juice of half an orange into the soup along with the yoghurt and blend. Garnish with parsley.

AVOCADO CREAM SOUP

1 onion - finely chopped
1 tsp butter
2 slices ginger - finely chopped
1/2 lemon
2 avocados
1 tsp ground coriander (or cumin or curry powder)
Freshly ground pepper
1/2 cup milk
1/2 cup chicken stock

Melt the butter in a saucepan, sauté the chopped onion until transparent and add the chopped ginger. Halve the avocados, rub each half with the lemon to stop browning and scoop out the flesh into a bowl. Sprinkle with the ground coriander. Pour the onion and ginger into a food processor or blender, add the avocados, pepper, milk and chicken stock and blend until smooth and creamy. If too thick, thin with water. Eat warm or chilled.

SWEETCORN SOUP

1 can cream-style corn
1 tsp butter
1 Tbsp chopped onion
1/2 red pepper - diced
1 Tbsp chopped green onion
1/2 cup milk
1 tsp freshly ground pepper
1/2 tsp salt
1 tsp curry powder

Melt the butter in a saucepan and add the chopped onion. Sauté until transparent and pour in the corn. Add the milk and pepper and stir. Bring the soup up to boil, turn down and simmer for 5-10 minutes. Add the diced red pepper and green onions, stir, cook for further 5 minutes and serve.

SHRIMP & CUCUMBER SOUP

1/2 cucumber - grated
3/4 can of shrimp or 4 oz fresh shrimp.
1 tsp dill
3-4 Tbsps yoghurt
Water

Blend all the above ingredients in blender or food processor. Serve cold garnished with the remaining shrimp and some fresh dill.

BORSCHT

1 tsp butter
1 cup beets (1 medium can)
1 tsp dill
1 Tbsp chopped parsley
1 clove garlic - chopped
Water or chicken stock to cover
Juice of an orange
1 Tbsp peeled, pearl onions
1/2 tsp salt
2 Tbsps yoghurt or sour cream

Melt the butter in a saucepan, add the beets and the dill and stir. Put in the parsley and garlic and add enough water or stock to cover the beets. Squeeze in the juice of an orange and add the pearl onions. Sprinkle with salt and cook over medium heat for about 10-15 minutes. Stir in the yoghurt or sour cream and serve.

CLAM CHOWDER

5-6 slices bacon - chopped
1 onion - chopped
2 potatoes - diced
2 cloves garlic - chopped
4-5 slices ginger
3 tomatoes - chopped
Freshly ground pepper
1 Tbsp chopped parsley
2 sticks celery - chopped
2 cans clams
1 tsp dill
Bay leaf
1 cup clam broth or water (if necessary)
Cherry tomatoes for garnish

Heat a large saucepan over a high heat and fry the bacon. Add the onions, potatoes, garlic, ginger and tomatoes and stir well. Continue with the parsley, pepper and celery and strain in the juice from the clams, reserving the clams for later. Put the lid on and simmer for 10-15 minutes, adding more liquid if necessary. Put in the bay leaf, clam juice and cherry tomatoes about 5 minutes before serving , add the clams 2 minutes before and serve as soon as they're heated through.

GAZPACHO

1 onion - chopped
2-3 cloves garlic - chopped
1 red pepper - chopped
1/2 green pepper - chopped
1 tomato - chopped
Freshly ground pepper
1 hot pepper
1/2 cucumber - chopped
1/2 tsp salt
Juice of 1/2 lemon
1/2 cup water

Blend all the above ingredients in a food processor or blender. Tear up a couple of pieces of bread and add to the soup. Blend for another minute and serve garnished with chopped green onions.

TOMATO & GIN SOUP

1 tsp butter
1 onion - chopped fine
1 small can tomatoes
1 tsp frozen orange juice
2 Tbsps light cream
2-4 Tbsps gin

Melt the butter in a saucepan and stir in the onions until they have softened. Pour in the tomatoes, stir and allow to melt. Add the orange juice, put the lid on and simmer for 10 minutes. Pour into a blender or food processor and blend. Add the cream and gin, stir and heat through gently for a few more minutes. Serve garnished with fresh mint leaves.

CURRIED PARSNIP SOUP

1 chopped onion
1/2 tsp butter
3-4 slices ginger - chopped
1 parsnip - peeled and grated
Freshly ground pepper
1 1/2 cups water
1 Tbsp julienned orange zest
Juice of 1/2 orange
1 tsp curry powder
Chopped parsley

Melt the butter in a saucepan, medium heat, and sweat (cook slowly, stirring frequently) the onion, ginger and parsnip until soft. Add the pepper, pour in the water and bring back to the boil. Turn down the heat and simmer, with the lid on for 15 minutes. Squeeze in the orange juice, add the orange zest and curry powder, stir well and simmer for a further 5 minutes. Serve dusted with chopped parsley.

HOT & SOUR SOUP

4 cups water
1 chicken breast - skinned & shredded
1 onion - chopped
1 carrot - chopped
1 Tbsp garlic - chopped
1 tomato - chopped
4 slices fresh ginger - julienned
Freshly ground pepper
4 dried Chinese mushrooms - soaked and sliced
1/2 packet firm tofu - cubed
1/2 red pepper - diced
3 hot peppers

Bring the water to the boil, put the lid on and simmer all the above ingredients for 10-15 minutes.

1 Tbsp cornstarch
1 tsp sesame oil
1 Tbsp vinegar
1 egg
Cilantro

Dissolve the cornstarch in a little water and stir into the soup. Add the sesame oil and vinegar. Put the lid back on and simmer for another 5 minutes. Beat the egg lightly in a bowl and beat it into the soup. Cook for a further 2 minutes and serve garnished with chopped cilantro.

ONION SOUP

1 Tbsp butter
2 onions - thinly sliced
6 whole cloves garlic
1 tsp thyme
1 cup red wine
1/2 tsp salt
1 Tbsp chopped parsley
1 tsp brown sugar

Melt the butter in a saucepan and caramelize the onion rings over a medium heat. Add the garlic, thyme, salt, 1/2 cup red wine and the brown sugar. Stir well, still boiling hard, and when it becomes sticky, pour in the other 1/2 cup red wine and the chopped parsley. Turn the heat down, put the lid on and simmer for 20 minutes.

TOMATO & DILL SOUP

6 large tomatoes - peeled & chopped
1 chicken stock cube

2 cups water
1 tsp dill
1 Tbsp freshly ground pepper
1 tsp sugar
2 Tbsps sugar
Handful of chopped parsley

Pour 2 cups water into a saucepan and bring all the ingredients to a boil. Simmer with the lid on for 15-20 minutes. Pour into a blender or food processor and blend until smooth. Stir in 2 Tbsps of cream and some chopped parsley and gently heat through. DO NOT BOIL. Serve hot or cold.

BASIC CHICKEN SOUP

1 chicken breast - chopped
2 cups boiling water
1 Tbsp chopped onion
Bay leaf
1 tsp oregano

Simmer all the above ingredients in a saucepan for 15-20 minutes.

AVGOLIMONO

Break 1 egg into a bowl and beat with a fork. Beat in the juice of a lemon and pour some Basic Chicken Soup into the mixture one teaspoon at a time until the egg mixture is warm. Add the egg mixture to the rest of the soup and add 1 cup of cooked rice. Heat through and serve, sprinkled with chopped parsley.

STRACCIATELLA

Break 1 egg into a bowl and beat with a fork. Pour the egg into the Basic Chicken Soup beating the soup all the time to produce strands of egg. Serve sprinkled with chopped parsley.

CABBAGE & POTATO SOUP

3-4 slices bacon - chopped
3 potatoes - diced
1/2 cabbage - cored & sliced crosswise
Freshly ground pepper

Fry the bacon in a saucepan over a high heat and stir in the potatoes. Add the cabbage and stir well to make sure everything is coated. Grind about 1 Tbsp pepper into the pan and pour in 3 cups of water. Bring to the boil, turn the heat down, put the lid on and simmer for 20-25 minutes. Serve with French bread.

FRYPAN MEAT SOUP

2 Tbsps oil
1 lb/500g ground beef
1 onion - chopped
1 carrot - grated
Bay leaf
1 tsp rosemary

1/2 tsp salt

Freshly ground pepper

1 Tbsp grated ginger

1/2 cup water

1 cup beer

1 carrot - sliced

6 pearl onions

1 Tbsp oil

Turn the frypan to 400 F/200 C and stir the meat into the hot oil. When it turns brown, add the onions and carrot and cook for a few minutes. Add the bay leaf, rosemary, salt, pepper and ginger and pour in the water and beer. Simmer. In a separate frypan cook the carrot slices and pearl onions over a high heat until they are toasty and brown. Add to the meat soup, put the lid on and simmer for 15 minutes.

PEANUT BUTTER SOUP

1 Tbsp oil

1 chopped onion

1 grated carrot

2 Tbsps peanut butter

1 can ginger ale

2 cloves chopped garlic

1 tsp curry powder

1 dozen cherry tomatoes

Heat the oil in a saucepan over high heat and sauté the onions until transparent. Add the grated carrot, garlic and peanut butter and stir until melted. Pour in the ginger ale and sprinkle with curry powder. Add the cherry tomatoes, turn the heat down and simmer with the lid on for 20-25 minutes. Squeeze a little lemon juice over and serve.

BEAN SOUP

2 Tbsps oil

1 onion - finely chopped

1 carrot - chopped

6 whole cloves garlic

1 bunch watercress - chopped

1 can cannellini beans & 1 can water

1 chorizo sausage - chopped

1 tsp dried chillies

1 tsp thyme

1 lemon

Heat the oil in a saucepan and brown the onions. Add the carrot, garlic and watercress and stir. Rinse the beans well and pour into the pan along with 1 can of water. Put in the sausage and chillies, bring back to the boil, turn the heat down and simmer with the lid on for 20 minutes. Stir in some thyme and lemon juice and serve.

HOT & SOUR SALAD SOUP

1 Tbsp oil

Leftover salad

2 cups water

Freshly ground pepper

1 Tbsp chopped parsley

1 chopped onion

6-7 cloves garlic - whole

2 Tbsps vinegar

1/2 tsp salt

Heat up the oil in a saucepan and tip in the leftover salad. Add the water, a lot of freshly ground pepper, parsley, onion and garlic and stir. Put the lid on, bring to the boil, turn the heat down and simmer for 15-20 minutes. For the last 5 minutes add the vinegar and salt. Strain and serve in a bowl garnished with croutons.

✒ CROUTONS

Slice some bread and cut into cubes. Heat up 2 Tbsps oil in a frypan and toss in the bread cubes. Stir and cook until crisp and brown or toss the bread cubes in oil and put on a baking tray in a 350 F /180 C oven for 10-15 minutes. Mix with 1 Tbsp chopped parsley and serve with soup.

BEER SOUP

3-4 cloves garlic - chopped

2 Tbsps olive oil

1 onion - finely chopped

Large hunk of stale bread

1 bottle beer

1 tsp caraway seeds

1/2 tsp oregano

1 cup hot water

1/2 tsp salt

Freshly ground pepper

Red pepper to garnish

Heat up a saucepan and sauté the onion and garlic in the hot oil. Tear the bread into small pieces and add to the pan. Stir well. When the bread has soaked up all the juices add the beer, water and seasonings. Put the lid on and simmer for 10-15 minutes over moderate heat. Serve garnished with strips of red pepper.

GARLIC & ALMOND SOUP

1 cup shelled almonds

6 cloves garlic

2 Tbsps olive oil

Juice of a lemon

1/2 tsp salt

Freshly ground pepper

1 1/2 cups water

1 bunch watercress or spinach

Blend all the above ingredients in a food processor or blender until smooth. Pour into a bowl, add a dash of sherry and serve well chilled.

COLD CUCUMBER SOUP

1 cucumber, chopped
1/2 cup toasted walnuts
1 cup apple juice
1 clove garlic, chopped
2 Tbsps fresh dill or 1 tsp dried
1/2 tsp salt
1 tsp pepper
2 Tbsps yoghurt

Mix all the above ingredients, except the yoghurt, in a food processor. Pour into a bowl, stir in the yoghurt and chill.

CORN SOUP (Adapted From The Chinese)

3 green onions, chopped
3-4 slices of ginger, julienned
2 Tbsps butter
Cilantro/parsley, chopped
1 tsp turmeric
1/2 tsp ground, black pepper
1 Tbsp soy sauce
2 cups water
1/2 tsp cornstarch mixed with 2 Tbsps sherry
1 packet frozen corn kernels

Cook the onion and ginger in the butter. Stir in the turmeric and corn until well coated and add black pepper and water or stock. Cook for 2 minutes. Add soy sauce, parsley or cilantro and the cornstarch mixture. Stir well and cook for 1 minute. Serve garnished with chopped green onions.

BLUEBERRY SOUP

2 cups fresh or frozen blueberries
1/3 cup concentrated, frozen orange juice
1 apple, cored and sliced
1 Tbsp lemon juice
1 Tbsp sugar
1 cup cider or sparkling wine

Blend all the ingredients in a blender or food processor and chill. Serve as a starter or dessert, garnished with mint leaves or edible flowers.

LENTIL & FRUIT SOUP (Armenian Style)

1/2 cup soaked lentils
1 ham bone
1 onion, quartered
2 carrots, quartered
2 sticks celery, quartered
1 clove garlic
1/2 tsp salt

Place the lentils in a saucepan and cover with 2 cups of cold water. Add all the ingredients, bring to a boil, cover and simmer for 25 minutes. Discard the bone and add the following ingredients:

2 potatoes, cubed
1 tsp black pepper
1/2 cup dried apricots
1/2 cup dried pitted prunes
1/3 cup walnuts, chopped
1 Tbsp butter
1 Tbsp oil
Chopped cilantro

Heat the oil and butter in a frypan and sauté the potatoes and black pepper. Add to the soup. Roughly chop the fruit and walnuts, by hand or in a food processor and add these to the soup. Simmer for 5-10 minutes more diluting if necessary with 1 cup of cranberry juice or water and serve sprinkled with chopped cilantro.

GREEN BEAN SOUP

1 packet frozen, sliced beans
1/2 medium onion, finely chopped
1 clove garlic, finely chopped
1 Tbsp butter
1 heaping Tbsp flour
4 cups water or apple juice
1 tsp summer savoury or thyme
Salt & pepper
Juice of 1/2 lemon
Handful blanched almonds

Cook onion and garlic in the butter. Stir in the flour and add the water or apple juice. Add beans and herbs, cook for 2 minutes and then blend. Season and add lemon juice. Fry almonds in butter and mix into the soup. Garnish with yoghurt and chopped parsley.

SHERRY CONSOMMÉ

1 can consommé
2 Tbsps sherry
Chopped green onion
Orange zest

Warm the consommé gently in a saucepan and pour into soup bowls. Stir in the sherry and decorate with thin rings of green onion and thin strips of orange zest.

SWISS CHEESE SOUP

2 slices toasted, French bread
4 Tbsps Swiss cheese, grated
1 cup milk
Salt & pepper
Nutmeg
1 Tbsp butter
Chopped parsley or chopped green onions

Put one slice of toast in a warm bowl. Sprinkle with cheese and top with another slice of toast to make a sandwich. Heat the milk gently in a saucepan and season with salt, pepper and nutmeg. Pour into the bowl, add the butter and garnish with sliced green onions or chopped parsley.

TURKEY SOUP WITH CHILLIED WALNUTS

1 cup turkey cubes
1 onion, chopped
1 tomato, chopped
3 slices of fresh ginger, julienned
1 tsp finely chopped orange zest
Salt & pepper
1 tsp thyme, sage or oregano
1 Tbsp butter or oil
2 cups cider (1 bottle)

Heat the butter in a saucepan and fry the ginger and onion. Add the chopped tomato, orange zest, oregano, salt and pepper and stir in the turkey cubes. Pour in the cider, cover and simmer for 20 minutes. Stir in the soy sauce and simmer a few minutes longer.

🐟 CHILLIED WALNUTS

1/2 cup walnuts, shelled & quartered
1/2 tsp cayenne pepper
1 clove garlic, crushed
1/2 tsp salt

Shake all the above ingredients well in a paper bag. Heat 2 Tbsps oil or butter and sauté the nuts. Remove and drain. Serve as a garnish for turkey soup.

GOLDEN PUMPKIN SOUP

3 green onions, finely sliced
2 Tbsps butter
1 cup grated carrot
1 tsp ground cumin
1 tsp ground ginger
2 cups cooked, mashed pumpkin or 1 can
1 can creamed corn
1/2 tsp salt
Freshly ground pepper
3 cups water, stock or apple juice

Melt the butter in a saucepan and put in the carrot, corn and pumpkin. Stir in the remaining ingredients and simmer for 8-10 minutes. Serve garnished with chopped green onion and croutons.

MEAT BALL SOUP

1/2 lb/250g ground pork
1 onion, finely chopped
1 tomato, quartered

1 bunch spinach or watercress

2-3 slices fresh ginger

1 Tbsp soy sauce

Pepper

Roll the pork into walnut sized balls. Boil 3 cups of water and drop in the balls. Add the onion, 1 tsp pepper, ginger, soy sauce and the tomato. Cut the stalks off the spinach or watercress, slice them crosswise and add to the soup. Cook for 10 minutes, then add the leaves of spinach or watercress. Cook 1 minute and serve.

CHILLED GUACAMOLE SOUP

2 avocados, halved & peeled

1 cup buttermilk

Juice of 1/2 lemon

1/2 tsp chilli peppers or few drops of tabasco

2 Tbsps chopped fresh cilantro

Purée all the above ingredients in a blender or food processor and serve chilled.

ALMOST INSTANT SHRIMP SOUP

3 Tbsps butter

1 med onion , chopped.

1 cup of frozen peas

2 cloves garlic, chopped

1 bunch cilantro or parsley, chopped coarsely

1 tsp curry powder

1 can shrimp

3 slices of orange zest, finely chopped

1 bottle beer

1/2 red pepper, chopped

Heat the butter and sauté the onion. Add the garlic, curry powder, orange zest and shrimp and stir well. Pour in the beer and season to taste with salt and pepper. Add the frozen packet of peas for the last 5 minutes and garnish with chopped red pepper and chopped parsley or cilantro.

NEW ORLEANS CLAM CHOWDER

2-3 slices bacon, chopped

2 Tbsps oil

1 onion, chopped

1 Tbsp flour

2 cloves garlic, chopped

1 or 2 hot peppers or 1 tsp chilli flakes or 1 tsp hot sauce

2 bay leaves

2 tsps paprika

1 potato, chopped

1 cup water or clam broth

2 or 3 tomatoes or 1 can tomatoes

1 celery stalk, chopped

1 tsp thyme

Salt & pepper
Hardboiled eggs
Toasted hazelnuts

Heat the oil in a large saucepan over a high heat and fry the bacon until crispy. Add the onions and 1 Tbsp of flour and stir to make a roux. Put in the whole tomatoes, garlic, celery, thyme, bay leaves, hot sauce and paprika. Stir well and add the potato, clams and the broth. Cover and simmer for 20 minutes. Garnish with hard boiled eggs and toasted hazelnuts and serve with slabs of bread for a hearty "knife and fork" soup.

DOG SOUP

1lb/500g any white fish, cut into pieces
1 Tbsp sea salt
3 Tbsps olive oil
2-3 cloves garlic
2 Tbsps chopped, green onions
3 1/2 cups boiling water
3/4 cup juice of oranges
1/4 cup cubed stale bread
Chopped parsley

Salt the fish and let stand for up to 30 minutes. Lightly brown the garlic cloves quickly in the oil and then discard them. Add the cubed bread and cook until brown. Boil the water and add the fish, piece by piece. Cook over high heat for 5 minutes. Just before serving, stir in the orange juice, green onions, sprinkle with chopped parsley and serve with the croutons.

SWEET PEPPER SOUP

1 red pepper, chopped
1 onion, chopped
2 tomatoes, chopped
Juice of 1 lemon
1 cup apple juice
1/2 tsp ground ginger
Salt & pepper
2 Tbsps olive oil

Heat the oil in a frypan and fry the onions until transparent. Stir in the peppers and tomatoes and add the rest of the ingredients. Put the lid on and simmer for 20-25 mins. Purée the mixture in a blender or food processor and serve.

CARIBBEAN CABBAGE SOUP

1/2 green cabbage, quartered, cored & sliced
2 Tbsps oil
3 slices fresh ginger, chopped fine or 1/2 tsp ground ginger
(this is one of the few recipes where the two kinds of ginger can be interchanged.)
1 medium onion , chopped
6 cups hot water
1 large potato, skin on, washed and diced
1/2lb/250g fresh shrimp (or 1 can) and 1 cup dried shrimp
1/2 tsp salt
1 tsp black pepper

Juice & zest of 1/2 lemon

1/2 tsp cayenne pepper

1/4 cup grated coconut

Soak the dried shrimp in white wine for 30 minutes. Heat the oil and fry the onion and ginger for 1 minute over medium heat. Add potatoes and toss until glistening. Stir in the cayenne pepper, salt and toss well until lightly browned. Add the cabbage, black pepper and the dried shrimp. Pour in the hot water and simmer for 5-10 minutes. Add the grated coconut, lemon juice and zest and for the last 1 minute of cooking add the fresh shrimp. Decorate with chopped green onion or chopped cilantro.

STALE BREAD SOUP

2 Tbsps olive oil

1 onion, chopped fine

6 cloves garlic, chopped

2 lbs/1 kg ripe tomatoes, or 1 can tomatoes

1 tsp black pepper

Salt

4-5 cups hot water

2 Tbsps fresh basil or 1 tsp dried basil or 1 tsp dried thyme

2 thick slices stale bread torn into pieces

1 bunch green onions or a handful of fresh basil leaves.

Fry onion in oil over medium heat until transparent. Stir in the pepper and garlic, cook 1 minute, add tomatoes and cook for further 5 minutes. Stir in the bread, salt and water, simmer 10 - 15 minutes, stirring occasionally. Serve hot garnished with thinly sliced green onions or chopped fresh basil.

OATMEAL SOUP

1 cup oatmeal

2 Tbsps butter

1 onion, chopped

1 packet frozen spinach, chopped

1 tsp curry powder

Juice of a lemon

1/2 tsp salt

1 tsp pepper

Melt the butter in a saucepan and sauté the oatmeal until brown and crispy. Add the onion and curry powder and toss well. Stir in the chopped, frozen spinach and pour 2 cups boiling water over. Season with salt, pepper and lemon juice and simmer for 8- 10 minutes. Serve hot with a swirl of sour cream and chopped parsley.

ANCHOVY SOUP

2 Tbsps olive oil

3-4 cloves garlic, chopped

1 or 2 cans anchovies

1 bunch chopped parsley

1 Tbsp tomato paste

2 slices bread, without crusts

4 cups hot water

1 tsp pepper
Parmesan cheese
4 slices bread

Fry garlic & anchovies in the olive oil for 3-4 minutes over medium heat or until the anchovies melt. Stir in the parsley, pepper, tomato paste and water. Bring to a boil, crumble in the bread, cover and simmer for 10 minutes. If preferred, blend soup in the blender or food processor. Sprinkle the rest of the bread slices with parmesan cheese and toast lightly. Pour the soup into bowls and float the toasted bread on top.

CRAB BISQUE

1 onion
1 Tbsp butter
2 slices ginger, chopped
1/2 tsp salt
1/2 tsp pepper
1/2 tsp dill
6 green onions, chopped
1 Tbsp tomato paste
2 cans crab
1/2 tsp sugar
1/2 cup thin cream
1 cup white wine

Melt the butter and sauté the onion. Add the ginger, green onions, salt, pepper, dill, tomato paste, crab and sugar and stir well. Pour in the cream and wine, heat through gently and serve hot.

CREAM OF MANGO SOUP

1 can mango or 1 fresh mango
2-3 slices fresh ginger, finely chopped or 1 tsp dried ginger
1 tsp toasted cumin seeds
1 cup yoghurt
Chopped basil or coriander
Juice of 1/2 lemon
1/2 tsp salt

Blend all the above ingredients and sprinkle with toasted cumin seeds and chopped basil or coriander. Serve cold.

APPETIZERS

CHEESE & ALMOND BALLS

1 cup/250g cream cheese
1/2 cup almonds
1 clove garlic, finely chopped
Toasted sesame seeds (black & white)
Juice of 1/4 lemon
1/4 tsp salt
1 tsp pepper

Lightly toast the almonds and mix together with the cheese, garlic, lemon juice, salt and pepper. Form into small balls and roll in toasted sesame seeds. Serve with toothpicks.

STUFFED EGGS

6 hard boiled eggs
2 Tbsps tomato ketchup
2 Tbsps cream or mayonnaise
1/2 tsp salt
1/2 tsp pepper

Halve the eggs and put the yolks into a bowl. Arrange the whites on a plate. Mix together the egg yolks, tomato ketchup, mayonnaise, salt and pepper and pile back into the whites. Garnish with chopped parsley.

PATÉ & ORANGE JUICE

Slice a large piece of paté and arrange on a bed of lettuce. Drizzle with the juice of half an orange and decorate with orange or mandarin slices.

SALMON PATÉ

1 can sockeye salmon
6 green onions
2 Tbsps butter
1 Tbsp fresh dill or 1 tsp dried

Blend all the above ingredients, chill and arrange on a plate with orange slices.

CLAMS DANIEL

1 Tbsp oil
1 Tbsp chopped onion
1 tsp freshly ground pepper
1 tsp curry powder
Juice of 1/2 lemon
1 Tbsp chopped parsley

2 cloves chopped garlic

1 can clams

2 Tbsps. sherry

Heat the oil in a frypan and sauté the onions until transparent. Add the curry powder, lemon juice, parsley and garlic. Stir well and add the clams. Stir for 1-2 minutes, add the sherry, set light to them and FLAMBÉ !

GRILLED TOMATO & CHEESE

1 firm tomato

1/2 tsp dry mustard

1/2 tsp dill

1/2 tsp hot red pepper

2 onion rings

1/2 cup of grated cheese & breadcrumbs

1 slice of bread

Toast one slice of bread and butter it. Thinly slice the tomato using a serrated edge knife and place an overlapping layer on the toast. Sprinkle with the dry mustard, hot pepper and dill, dot with butter, place the thin onion rings on top and place in the toaster oven on broil. When the mixture is hot, coat with the mixture of cheese and breadcrumbs and replace in the oven until nicely browned and bubbling.

APRICOTS & BLUE CHEESE

Fresh apricots

Blue cheese

Halve an apricot and remove the stone. Put 1 tsp blue cheese into one half and press the two halves together. Keep together with a toothpick or fancy umbrella. Repeat with as many apricots as necessary.

GRILLED GRAPEFRUIT

Halve a grapefruit. Place on a plate and sprinkle with some brown sugar. Place in the toaster oven on broil and cook until the sugar is bubbling. Serve immediately.

CHICKPEA VINAIGRETTE

1 can chickpeas, washed & drained

Juice of 1/2 orange

Chopped parsley

Salt & pepper

Mix all the above ingredients together, garnish with more chopped parsley and serve with pita bread and tzatziki.

✦ TZATZIKI

1 zucchini or cucumber

Yoghurt

1/2 tsp salt

1/2 tsp pepper

1/2 tsp oregano or dill

Grate the zucchini or cucumber and stir into the yoghurt. Add salt & pepper and a little oregano or dill.

GUACAMOLE ONE

Halve an avocado and rub with lemon juice to prevent browning. Mash with some chopped green onion and the juice of 1/2 lemon.

GUACAMOLE TWO

1 avocado, peeled & mashed
2 tomatoes, seeded & chopped
2 Tbsps chopped cilantro
Juice of 1/2 lemon
1 clove of garlic - optional
Few drops of hot sauce, to taste

Mix all the above ingredients together and serve with tortilla chips.

SOUR CREAM DIP

Mix 3-4 Tbsps sour cream with some chopped green onion and a few drops of hot sauce.

BEAN DIPS

1 can chick peas
1/2 onion
1 tsp chilli powder
2 cloves garlic
1 tsp ground cumin
1/2 tsp salt
1 tsp pepper
2 tomatoes
1 bunch parsley
1/2 cup yoghurt

Blend all the above ingredients in a food processor.

1 can red kidney beans
1 bunch green onions
1 clove garlic
2 Tbsps olive oil
1/2 cup yoghurt
1/2 tsp salt
1 tsp pepper
1 avocado, optional

Blend all the above ingredients in a food processor and serve both dips with tortilla chips or as an alternative, spread the dip onto thin slices of bread and roll up, using tooth picks if necessary. Chill and then slice and place under the broiler to crisp up. Serve hot.

SALSA

1/2 yellow pepper
1/2 red pepper
1/2 green pepper
1 Tbsp finely chopped onion
1/2 tsp cayenne pepper
1 Tbsp oil
1/2 ear fresh corn
1 Tbsp chopped parsley
1 Tbsp chopped green onion
1 tsp vinegar
1/2 tsp sugar

Cut the peppers into strips and chop finely. Mix with the remaining ingredients and toss well.

SPICY CHICKEN WINGS

Chicken wings, cut across at joints, tips discarded or used for stock
3-4 cloves garlic - finely chopped
2 Tbsps brown sugar
1 Tbsp dry mustard
1/2 bottle beer
1 Tbsp sesame oil
1 Tbsp soy sauce
1 tsp vinegar
Sesame seeds

Heat up a dry frypan over high heat. Lay in the chicken wings and brown lightly on each side. Turn the heat down to medium and stir in the garlic, brown sugar, mustard and beer. Cook for 5-8 minutes making sure the chicken wings are well coated with the sauce. Add the sesame oil, soy sauce and vinegar, stir well and cook for a further 5 minutes. Add more beer if the sauce gets too thick. Serve on a platter sprinkled with sesame seeds and chopped parsley.

MUSHROOM ANTIPASTO

Take a bowl and half-fill with whole, fresh mushrooms. Sprinkle with 1/2 tsp salt. Mix in a few onion rings, green and black olives, 2 Tbsps olive oil, freshly ground pepper and a can of tuna. Allow to marinate for 10 - 15 minutes and serve sprinkled with chopped green onions.

CUCUMBER & SHRIMP CUPS

1 cucumber
Yoghurt
Shrimp - canned or fresh
Prawn tails to decorate
Dill

Cut the cucumber into 2" slices and hollow out each one with a small spoon, leaving the bottom intact. Fill each cavity with some yoghurt and shrimp and serve garnished with prawn tails and fresh dill.

QUICK PIZZA DOUGH ONE

Thaw some frozen bread dough, break a piece off and knead it on a floured board. Roll out to the required size and bake in a 400 F/200 C oven for 10-12 minutes, with your preferred topping, or cook in a frypan for 5 minutes each side.

QUICK PIZZA DOUGH TWO

1 cup flour
Pinch salt
1 Tbsp baking powder
1 Tbsp grated cheddar cheese
1 tsp oregano
1 Tbsp chopped onion
1/2 cup water or to make a stiffish dough

Mix all the above ingredients together and knead on a floured board. Heat 1 Tbsp oil in a frypan, roll out the dough to the required size and pat down into the hot pan. Cook for 5 minutes, top with whatever you wish, flip over and cook for a further 5 minutes.

🖋 BASIC TOPPING

1 Tbsp tomato sauce
Few onion rings
3-4 anchovy fillets
1 clove chopped garlic
1 Tbsp mozzarella cheese

BACON & CLAMS QUICK PIZZA

3-4 slices bacon - chopped
1 tsp oregano
Freshly ground pepper
1 Tbsp chopped onion
2 Tbsps canned clams, juice reserved
1 Tbsp tomato sauce
Quick pizza dough one or two

Fry the bacon, oregano and pepper. Place the dough on top and when the underside is cooked, flip over and add the onions, clams and tomato sauce. Cook for further 5 minutes and flip over when done to brown. Serve. The clam juice? Pour into glasses, add a shot of vodka (or rum in Newfoundland), sprinkle with red pepper.

FRENCH ONION QUICK PIZZA

2 Tbsps oil
Onion rings
1 tsp dried chillies
3 cloves chopped garlic
Quick pizza dough one or two

Fry the onion rings in the oil until soft and brown. Add the dough on top and cook for 5 minutes. Flip over and brown the other side. Serve.

CHICORY, BLACK OLIVE & FETA

4-6 chicory heads
1 Tbsp olive oil
Black olives
Feta cheese
Freshly ground pepper

Quarter the chicory heads lengthwise and remove the cores. Arrange on a plate with a handful of black olives and some slices of feta cheese. Sprinkle with pepper and olive oil.

CARROT RAPEE

1 carrot - grated
1 Tbsp chopped parsley
1 tsp dill
Pinch of salt
1 Tbsp yoghurt

Mix all the above ingredients together well and serve.

BROCCOLI ANTIPASTO

2 Tbsps olive oil
1/3 cup white wine
1 head of broccoli - broken into florets
1/2 tsp salt

Heat the oil and wine in a frypan and put in the broccoli florets. Sprinkle with salt, put the lid on and simmer for 2 minutes. Drain and turn onto a large platter. Add cherry tomatoes, halved and tossed in olive oil, salt and basil. Add green olives sprinkled with chopped orange zest and garnish with black olives.

BRUSCHETTA

Slice French bread diagonally and crisp in the oven or toast. Rub each slice with a peeled garlic clove and drizzle a little olive oil over the top. Garnish with either an anchovy fillet and chopped parsley, or some slices of mozzarella or parmesan cheese and place under the broiler quickly, or leave plain.

PORK TAPAS

2 quick-fry, lean pork chops or thin slices of pork tenderloin
1 Tbsp paprika
2-3 Tbsps vinegar
2 Tbsps oil
1 red pepper - chopped
1/2 onion - thinly sliced
Freshly ground pepper

Marinate the pork in the paprika and vinegar for 15 minutes. Heat up frypan, with no oil, over a high heat. Fry for 5 minutes, turning once, remove and keep warm. Heat the oil in the pan and fry the red peppers, onion rings and freshly ground pepper for 2-3 minutes or until shiny. Tip onto a plate and arrange the pork on the top. Garnish with chopped parsley.

DEVILS ON HORSEBACK

Wrap a prune in a piece of bacon and poke 2 toothpicks through. Fry in a hot pan until the bacon is crisp. Serve as a savoury instead of dessert.

CHICKEN LIVERS

2 Tbsps flour

4-5 Tbsp butter

1 lb chicken livers

1 tsp thyme

Freshly ground pepper

1 chopped onion

3-4 cloves garlic - chopped

1/4 cup brandy

Flour the chicken livers in a plastic bag. Melt the butter in a frypan and immediately stir in the chicken livers and thyme. When the outsides are golden and crisp, add the chopped onion and garlic and cook for 5-6 minutes. Pour in the brandy and blend the mixture in a food processor or blender until smooth. Serve with melba toast (thin slices of bread allowed to dry out in a 200 F/100 C oven) or put in a small bowl, top with clarified butter and wrap in cellophane as a gift!

TEA EGGS

6 eggs

1 Tbsp salt

1 Tbsp soy sauce

3 star anise

Black tea to cover

Boil the eggs for 20 minutes. When cool, pour out the water and tap the eggs gently with a spoon until they are cracked all over. Return the eggs to the pan, cover with hot, black tea and add the salt, soy and anise. Bring back to the boil, lower the heat and simmer for 1 hour. Turn off the heat and leave in the liquid for 8 hours. Remove shells just before serving.

MARINATED MUSHROOMS

Fresh, small mushrooms (enough to fill a pickle jar)

2 Tbsps olive oil

1/2 tsp salt

1 tsp pepper

Juice of a lemon

1 tsp tarragon

Put the mushrooms into the jar. Add the olive oil, lemon juice, salt, pepper and tarragon. Put the lid on, shake well and leave for 30 minutes.

MUSHROOM & MINT

1 Tbsp butter

1/2 onion - thinly sliced

| 1/2 lb mushrooms |
| 1/2 tsp salt |
| Freshly ground pepper |
| 1 Tbsp mint |

Melt the butter in a frypan and add the onions. Toss lightly and cook for 2 minutes. Stir in the mushrooms, salt, pepper and mint and cook for 2 more minutes or until the mushrooms are slightly coloured but NOT OVERCOOKED. Serve with a squeeze of lemon juice over the top and some chopped parsley.

CEVICHE

| 1 fillet of white fish (e.g. halibut, snapper etc.) |
| 1 lime |
| 1/2 - 1 tsp dried hot chillies |
| Few shrimps |

Cut the fish fillet into the thinnest slices you can and combine in a bowl with the lime juice, dried chillies and some shrimp. Leave marinating for 15 to 30 minutes until the fish turns opaque and serve chilled.

EGG IN A NEST

| 1 egg |
| 1 slice of bread |
| Salt & pepper |

Cut a circle out of the slice of bread with a wine glass and fry the bread (and the circle) on one side. Turn over and break an egg into the hole. Sprinkle with a little salt, pepper and paprika and cook until the white is set. Serve with the cut-out circle propped up against the side with a toothpick through it and some cherry tomatoes or asparagus quickly sautéed in hot oil for a minute. Garnish with chopped parsley.

TURNIP OR RUTABAGA APPETIZER

| 1 or 2 rutabagas or yellow turnips (some call them wurzels), peeled. |
| 1 Tbsp soy sauce |
| 1 Tbsp oil |
| 1 Tbsp rye whiskey |
| 1 tsp sugar |
| 1 tsp tarragon |
| 1/2 tsp salt |

Halve the turnips and slice thinly. Take the slices, stack them up and cut into julienne strips. Make the dressing by mixing the remaining ingredients together well. Arrange the turnip sticks on a plate and pour over the dressing. Leave to marinate for 20 minutes to 1 hour and garnish with edible flowers.

SARDINE & GREEN ONION SANDWICH

Butter some slices of bread and put a can of sardines on one slice. Cut the green onions in half, slice lengthwise and lay diagonally across the sardines. Top with the other slice of bread, cut into lengths and serve.

MARMITE & CUCUMBER SANDWICH, (The Queen's Favorite)

Take a cucumber, drag a fork down the outside all the way round and slice very thinly (the edges will be serrated). Cut very thin slices of bread and spread with a little butter. Put a thin layer of marmite on one slice, lay the cucumber slices on top and put another slice of bread on top. Cut into triangles and serve.

DARK RYE & CREAM CHEESE SANDWICH

Spread 4 or 5 slices of dark rye bread with cream cheese, making sure you spread it right to the edges. Stack up the slices, trim the edges and cut into 3 or 4 lengths. Turn over onto the side and cut each length into neat squares. Arrange the cubes on a plate.

MINCEMEAT & PEANUT BUTTER WHEELS

Cut the end off a loaf making sure the loaf remaining is shorter than the knife. Put the blade into the bread and cut round inside the crust, back and forwards and spiralling into the centre. Roll the middle out gently and you will have a large rectangle of bread. Spread with some peanut butter and mincemeat, slip some orange inside and roll up. Cut crosswise into pinwheels and serve with orange slices.

HIYA-YAKO

1 packet firm tofu
Pickled ginger
Sliced green onions
Shaved bonito (dried fish flakes)
Few fresh shrimp or 1 can shrimp
Soy sauce

Cube the tofu and arrange on a bed of ice. Serve the rest of the ingredients in small bowls around it or sprinkle over the top. Serve the soy sauce separately and eat with chopsticks.

SALMON RAMEKINS

3/4 cup/200 g can salmon, drained and flaked
2 eggs
3 green onions, finely chopped
1 1/4 cup of milk
2 Tbsp julienned fresh ginger root
4 Tbsp cream
1 tsp fresh or dried dill, chopped fine

Lightly grease 4 ramekins and put a layer of chopped onions in the bottom of each one. Put 1 tsp of salmon on top of each. Beat the eggs and cream together, warm the milk and ginger in a saucepan and stir in to the egg mixture. Add salt and pepper and pour it all over the salmon. Sprinkle with dill and put the ramekins into a baking dish with water 1/3 way up the ramekin or cup. Bake 25 -30 minutes in a 350F/180C oven. Serve in the cup or turn out and decorate.

TOMATO ICE CREAM

1/2 lb/225 g fresh tomatoes, peeled & chopped
Juice of 1/2 lemon
Salt & pepper
1/2 cup whipped cream

Pulp the tomatoes, lemon juice, salt and black pepper in a food processor or blender. Fold in the cream and spoon into an ice-tray. Freeze for about an hour, it needs to be creamy and soft, not completely frozen. Serve as an appetizer with fresh basil or parsley.

CORN FRITTERS

1 fresh corn on the cob
1 onion, chopped
1 Tbsp flour
2 eggs
1 tsp baking powder
Salt & pepper
Small piece of spicy sausage, chopped fine or 1/2 tsp chilli pepper flakes
1 tsp dill
1-2 Tbsps oil or bacon fat

Scrape the corn off the cob. Put the onion and sausage in the food processor with the eggs, baking powder, flour, dill, salt and pepper and mix well. Empty into a bowl and stir the corn kernels into the mixture. Form into cakes and fry in oil or bacon fat until browned on each side.

CURRIED PEANUTS

Heat some raw peanuts in a dry frypan until hot. Pour in 1 Tbsp oil and 1 tsp curry powder. Shake well, turn the heat down and when browned, tip out onto a paper towel, sprinkle with salt and serve in a bowl.

SPICY ALMONDS

Heat some almonds in a dry frypan until hot. Pour in 1 Tbsp oil and 1/2 tsp cayenne. Shake well, turn the heat down and when browned, tip out onto a paper towel, sprinkle with salt and serve in a bowl.

BASQUE CUCUMBERS

1 cucumber
1 tsp sugar
3 rashers bacon
1 red onion, chopped
2 Tbsp vinegar
Juice of 1 orange
1 orange, peeled & sliced
Salt & pepper

Peel the cucumber and halve crosswise. Remove the seeds, slice into rounds and sprinkle with sugar. Fry the bacon until crisp, remove from the pan and pour off all the fat except about 2 Tbsps. Sauté the chopped onion in the fat for 1 minute. Add the cucumber, vinegar and orange juice. Stir and cook until the liquid has almost gone. Add salt & pepper and stir in the orange slices. Sprinkle with the crumbled bacon slices.

POUNTI

10 pitted prunes
1/2 lb/250g sausage meat or ground pork
1 medium onion, chopped
Chopped parsley
1/2 tsp dried thyme
1/2 cup plain flour
2-3 Tbsps milk
3 eggs
1 tsp pepper
1 tsp salt

Beat the eggs lightly first, put into the food processor with the rest of the ingredients, leaving the flour until last and process quickly. Make into small sausage-like rolls and fry.

GROUND LAMB BALLS WITH CHERRIES

1 lb/500g ground lamb
1/2 tsp nutmeg
1/2 tsp ground cloves
1/2 tsp ground cinnamon
1/2 lb/250g pitted cherries, fresh or canned
Juice of 1/2 lemon
1/2 tsp sugar, if fresh cherries
1 tsp orange zest
Salt & pepper
2 Tbsps olive oil

Mix the meat and spices together with your hands until it is smooth. Make into small balls and fry them gently in the oil until golden brown. Heat the cherries in a saucepan with the lemon juice, orange zest and sugar, if using. Add the sautéed meatballs and simmer gently. Add more liquid if necessary. Serve with pita bread.

FEGATO ALLA VENEZIANA

3/4lb/350g calves liver
2 Tbsps butter
2 Tbsps oil
2 onions, thinly sliced
2 Tbsps lemon juice
Salt & pepper
Chopped sage

Fry the onions in oil and butter and cook over medium heat until they're soft. Cut the liver into thin slivers, and add to the pan with the heat turned up high. Cook, at most 3 minutes, then add chopped sage, salt, pepper and lemon juice and cook one more minute (liver has to be eaten at once or it becomes tough). Decorate with fresh sage leaves.

MELITZANO

1 eggplant
1 chopped onion
1 tsp oregano
2 Tbsps olive oil
1 clove of garlic - optional

Bake the eggplant in a moderate oven for 45 minutes or until soft. Slit down the middle and scoop out the flesh into a food processor or blender. Blend with the onion, oregano (garlic) and olive oil. Serve in a bowl with pita bread.

CHICKEN HEARTS

1 lb/500g chicken hearts.
2 Tbsp vegetable oil
1/2 onion, chopped
3 slices fresh ginger, chopped
2 cloves garlic, chopped
1 tsp hot red cayenne pepper
1 tsp sesame oil
2 Tbsp soy sauce
1 Tbsp vinegar
1 Tbsp sugar
Salt & pepper
2 Tbsps brandy
Chopped parsley

Heat the oil in a frypan over medium heat. Add the onion, ginger, garlic and lots of black pepper. Stir well. Add the hearts, red pepper, sugar, brandy, soy sauce and vinegar. Heat to bubbling, stirring continuously, and cook 4 minutes. The sauce in the pan should be thick and sticky. If it gets too thick, add a Tbsp or two of water. Stir in sesame oil, add a handful of chopped parsley and serve with toothpicks as a snack or on rice as a main course.

PRAWNS IN BEER

Fresh, uncooked prawns with their shells on
1 bottle of beer
1 Tbsp fresh dill or dried
1 or 2 fresh fennel bulbs

About 1 hour before cooking, put the prawns into a bowl with the beer and dill and allow to marinate. Heat a frypan, with no oil, until very hot. Remove the prawns from the marinade and place in the dry pan. Sear until their skins change colour, about 1 minute each side. Meanwhile, heat 1 Tbsp oil in another pan. Slice the fennel and sauté the slices until browned on each side. Serve with the prawns and garnish with lemon wedges and freshly ground black pepper.

CHESTNUTS

Buy fat, shiny chestnuts, cut a cross on the side of each one and roast on the stove top or open fire. Eat with butter and salt.
For boiling, score round the middle of each chestnut with a knife and put into boiling water. Cook for 15-20 minutes

and peel immediately.
For dry chestnuts, soak in white wine for 24 hours and then cook for 20 minutes in boiling water.

CAMEMBERT ICE CREAM

1 large piece of camembert, not too ripe
1/2 - 3/4 cup cream
1/2 tsp cayenne pepper or tabasco
1/2 tsp salt

Blend the cheese and cream in a food processor. Season with cayenne pepper and salt. Freeze until firm but not hard. Serve with crackers.

PINEAPPLE, CELERY & SMOKED SAUSAGE SALAD

1 head of celery, chopped
1/2 medium-sized pineapple
1/4 lb/150g smoked sausage, sliced
1/4 cup/50g pecans, walnuts or almonds
2-3 Tbsps mayonnaise
Salt & pepper

Lightly roast the nuts in a frypan. Peel and core the pineapple and chop. Mix the ingredients together and serve.

JAPANESE ORANGE APPETIZER

1 orange
1 red onion
1 cup chopped cilantro
Juice of 1 lime
1/2 tsp cayenne pepper
1/4 cup olive oil
1 clove garlic, crushed (optional)
Salt & pepper

Peel and cut the orange crosswise into 4 thick pieces. Peel and slice the onion crosswise into 12 very thin slices. Lay the bottom slice of the orange on a plate, place an onion slice on top and then some chopped cilantro. Continue the layers. Mix the lime, cayenne, olive oil, garlic, salt and pepper and pour this dressing over the orange.

TAPENADE

1 cup black olives, stoned
2-3 Tbsps capers, drained
1 can anchovy fillets
1 can tuna fish (optional)
1 Tbsp mustard
1/2 cup olive oil
2 Tbsps brandy
1/2 tsp pepper
Handful chopped parsley

Blend all the ingredients in a food processor serve with crostini or focaccia.

ALMEJAS EL FARO (Clams in Sherry Sauce)

2 Tbsps olive oil
1 onion, sliced in rings
2 cloves garlic, chopped
1/2 cup cubed, cured ham or smoked sausage
1 large glass Spanish sherry
2 dozen clams and or 1 can clams
Chopped parsley
1 tsp black pepper
1/2 tsp salt

Heat the oil in a frypan and sauté the onions until light brown. Add the ham and garlic and stir well, then add the clams and chopped parsley. Pour in the sherry, add the salt, cover and cook for 3-4 minutes until the clams open. Sprinkle with black pepper and serve with chopped parsley.

CHICKEN & MANDARIN

1 chicken breast, cut into bite-sized pieces
1 Tbsp mandarin orange peel
1 mandarin orange
1 tsp pepper
1/2 tsp salt
1/4 onion, chopped
1 Tbsp oil

Heat the oil in a frypan and fry the chicken pieces over high heat. Add the mandarin peel, pepper and salt and stir well until the chicken has browned. Add the mandarin segments and chopped onion and cook for a further 5 minutes. Serve hot.

CAPONATINA

3/4 cup whole, blanched almonds
1-2 Tbsps olive oil
1/2 cup breadcrumbs
1 tin anchovies
1/2 cup orange juice
1 Tbsp sugar
1/4 cup vinegar
1/3 cup grated, bitter chocolate

Brown the almonds in the oil and drain. Add to the rest of the ingredients and purée in a blender or food processor. Pour over a pyramid of raw vegetables and decorate with prawns and hard-boiled eggs. As an alternative, heat the puréed sauce in a pan and pour over the vegetables for a warm salad.

SIDES

MASHED POTATOES

Using a fork, mash the potatoes with lots of pepper, some salt, 1 Tbsp of butter and some parsley. DON'T add milk or cream, and don't be shy about leaving a few small lumps. And once again, be generous with the pepper.

BUBBLE & SQUEAK

2 cups leftover brussel sprouts
2 cups leftover roast or mashed potatoes
1 Tbsp freshly ground pepper
1 egg - beaten
1 Tbsp oil

Heat the oil in a frypan. Chop the sprouts and potatoes and put in a large bowl. Sprinkle with the pepper, add the beaten egg and toss it all. Tip the mixture into the frypan and pat down into a cake. When the underneath has browned, place a plate over the top and flip the cake out onto the plate. Slide it back into the pan and cook the other side.

COLCANNON

Mashed potatoes
Boiled or steamed cabbage
Butter
Pepper & salt

Chop the cabbage very small and mix thoroughly with the mashed potatoes, 1 Tbsp pepper and a pinch of salt. Melt 1 Tbsp butter in a frypan and spoon in the mixture, pat down and gently heat through until a crust forms on the bottom. Serve with chopped parsley.

BASIC BECHAMEL OR WHITE SAUCE

4 Tbsp butter
3 Tbsp flour
1 cup milk or cream
1/2 tsp salt
Freshly ground pepper
1/2 tsp freshly grated nutmeg

Melt the butter in a saucepan then stir in the flour over a low heat for 2-3 minutes to make a roux. Add the milk or cream and whisk it smooth. Cook for few minutes until the sauce thickens. Add 1 Tbsp chopped parsley for a parsley sauce and pour over chicken or fish.

✒ ONION SAUCE

Cook 1/2 finely chopped onion in the butter and then add the flour and continue as above.

🐟 TOMATO SAUCE OR SAUCE HUSSARD

Add 1 Tbsp tomato paste to the basic bechamel sauce and simmer well. More chopped parsley can be added.

🐟 EGG SAUCE

Add 2 chopped hard-boiled eggs to the basic bechamel sauce and stir. Some chopped green onions can be added. Especially good served over asparagus.

🐟 CHEESE SAUCE

Add 1 Tbsp grated cheese and 1 tsp paprika to the basic bechamel sauce. Good served over some blanched broccoli.

BROCCOLI AU GRATIN

Grease a small gratin dish. Lay in some blanched broccoli, pour over the cheese sauce (above) and sprinkle 1 Tbsp breadcrumbs over the top. Broil for 2-3 minutes until crisp and brown.

PICKLED GINGER

Put some peeled slices of ginger into a bowl. Sprinkle with a little salt and sugar and 1-2 tsps of rice vinegar. Allow to stand for at least 20 minutes and serve as a side garnish.

SKORDALIA

4 slices white bread, without crusts
3 cloves garlic, chopped
2 potatoes, cooked
1/4 tsp salt
1/3 cup olive oil
Juice of 1 lemon (or 2 Tbsps vinegar)
1 tsp pepper

Put all the ingredients into a food processor and blend until a thick sauce. Serve with peeled and sliced broccoli stems - or any other fresh vegetables!

TERIYAKI SAUCE

2 Tbsps oil
1 Tbsp soy sauce
1 tsp sugar
1/2 tsp cayenne pepper (optional)

Heat up a frypan over medium heat and pour in the oil. Then pour the soy sauce into the middle of the pool of oil. Add the sugar in the middle of this and stir. Put in bite-sized pieces of fish (e.g.salmon or halibut), chicken or meatballs and fry until golden brown and caramelized, about 5 minutes. Serve garnished with green onion.

CHEESE STRAWS

Thaw a packet of frozen puff pastry and roll out with some grated cheese. Fold over a couple of times, adding a little cheese at each turn , and roll thin. Cut out into shapes, sprinkle with a little paprika and bake in the oven at 450 F/220 C for about 10 mins or until puffed up and golden brown.

BASIC BANNOCK

2 cups flour
1 Tbsp baking powder
3 Tbsps oil
Pinch salt
Water, milk, apple juice or beer to make a stiffish dough

Mix all ingredients together, pat out the dough to about 1/2" thickness and fry it, bake it (in a medium/hot oven) or throw it on a barbecue that isn't too hot. If you want to make "snake bread" , tear a piece off, roll out into a sausage and wind round a wooden spoon or stick and cook over a flame. For kids, tear off a small ball and make a 'helmet' of it round the top of a stick and cook it over a flame. Push butter and jam into the small hole and eat!

BANNOCK CAKE

Add to the basic bannock recipe :

3 eggs
2 Tbsps sugar
2 Tbsps currants
1 Tbsp chocolate chips

Mix all the ingredients, put into a cake tin and bake in a 375 F/190 C oven for about 15 minutes or put into an electric frypan at 375 F/190 C for about 15 minutes. For a pineapple upside-down cake, omit the currants & chocolate chips and lay some crushed pineapple in the bottom of the cake tin. Pour on the cake mixture and bake in the oven. To serve turn it over onto a plate.

FRUIT SCONE

Add 1 tsp sugar and 1/2 cup of currants to the basic bannock recipe and cook as above.

CHEESE BISCUIT

Add 1 cup grated cheese to the basic bannock recipe and cook as above.

PAN-FRIED LOAF

2 cups flour
1 Tbsp baking powder
3 Tbsp oil
1 egg
Pinch of salt
Water, milk, apple juice to make a stiffish dough

For kids, just mix some flour, baking powder, an egg, some oil and enough water, milk, apple juice, 7-up or whatever they want, to make a stiffish dough. Make a hole in the middle and fry in a dry pan for about 5-10 minutes. Turn, and cook the other side.

QUICK GARLIC & OLIVE FOCACCIA

2 cups flour
1 tsp salt
1 Tbsp baking powder
5-6 Tbsps olive oil
2/3-3/4 cup water or milk
2 cloves garlic, chopped
1 tsp dried rosemary or fresh
Grated parmesan cheese

Sift the flour, salt and baking powder together. Stir in the olive oil and garlic and add the water or milk to make a dough. Turn out onto a floured board and knead gently. Roll out and pat onto an ungreased 8" round flat pizza dish or baking tray. Poke holes all over with your fingers. Drizzle with a little olive oil and some grated parmesan cheese and bake for 12-15 minutes in a 400F/200C oven. Serve with chopped black olives in the indentations and dip in olive oil and balsamic vinegar.

SKILLET CORN BREAD

3/4 cup flour
1 1/4 cups cornmeal
2 Tbsps baking powder
2 eggs
1 cup milk
1 tsp salt
2 Tbsps sugar
2 Tbsps melted butter
1 can jalapenos - optional

Mix the flour, cornmeal and baking powder together. Break the eggs into a bowl and beat in the milk, salt, sugar and melted butter and add to the flour. Add some chopped jalapenos if using. Heat up a skillet and pour in the corn mixture. Put a lid on and cook for about 15-20 minutes over medium heat, flipping to cook the other side. Serve cut into wedges.

CORN BREAD

1 egg
2 Tbsps melted butter
1 cup white flour
2 Tbsps baking powder
1 cup cornmeal
1/2 cup fresh (or defrosted frozen) corn kernels
1/2 cup chopped chives, green onions or parsley

Whisk the egg and butter together, and in another bowl mix flour, cornmeal and baking powder. Stir the corn kernels into the flour mixture then stir all together with egg mixture. Whip until smooth. Pour it all into a flat cake pan and cook at 425F/200C for 20 minutes. Eat warm.

CORN BREAD & MAPLE SYRUP

Make corn bread as above (omitting the jalapeno peppers) and serve, cut in wedges, with ice cream and drizzled with maple syrup.

BEAN CAKE (Or A Type Of Johnnycake)

1 cup cooked beans
1 cup cornmeal
1/2 cup milk or water.
1 egg beaten
4 green onions, sliced thin
2 Tbsps oil
Salt and pepper

Mash up the beans in a bowl and mix with the cornmeal, milk, eggs, green onion, salt and pepper. Form into small cakes and fry in the hot oil for a couple of minutes or until lightly browned on each side. Eat with bacon or ham and maple syrup.

IRISH SODA BREAD

3/4 cup wholemeal flour
3/4 cup white flour
1/2 tsp salt
1 Tbsp butter
1 1/2 tsps baking soda
3 level tsps cream of tartar
1 tsp sugar
1/2 cup buttermilk

Mix together the flours, baking soda, cream of tartar, sugar and salt. Rub in the butter until the mixture resembles breadcrumbs. Pour in the buttermilk and knead into a dough. Shape into a ball, flatten slightly and cut into quarters. Dust lightly with flour and bake in a 450F/220C oven for 25-30 minutes.

POTATOES IN BASIL CREAM

1 lb/500g small potatoes, washed
1 thumb-sized piece of ginger, grated
3/4 cup cream
1 bunch fresh basil, sliced
1/2 tsp salt
1/2 tsp pepper

Boil the potatoes in salted water until tender, about 15 minutes. Meanwhile, gently simmer the ginger, cream, basil, salt & pepper in a small pan until thickened and aromatic. Pour onto a plate and arrange the hot potatoes on the sauce. Drizzle with a little more sauce and garnish with fresh basil.

ITALIAN STYLE POTATOES WITH SAGE

2 medium potatoes - cut into chunks
1 onion - roughly chopped

4 whole cloves of garlic - unpeeled
2 Tbsp olive oil
Sage - good handful of fresh, or 1 tsp dried

Heat the oil in a small frypan. Add the potato chunks and stir, coating them with the hot oil. Add the whole cloves of garlic and the sage. Put the lid on, turn the heat down and simmer for about 10 minutes, stirring occasionally. Stir in the chopped onion, and cook, lid on, another 10 minutes.

RISOTTO

2 Tbsps butter
2 Tbsps olive oil
1 onion - finely chopped
1 cup arborio, or short grain, rice
1 cup chicken stock
1 cup dry, white wine
1 grated carrot
2 Tbsps chopped parsley
1/2 tsp ground saffron
Parmesan cheese

Melt the butter and oil in a pan and sauté the onion until transparent. Add the arborio rice and stir until each grain of rice has absorbed the butter and oil. When golden brown slowly start adding the stock and wine, 1/4 cup at a time, until the risotto is smooth and creamy but with each grain of rice still separate, about 25 minutes. Towards the end of the cooking time, stir in the grated carrot, the saffron and 1 Tbsp chopped parsley. Serve garnished with parmesan cheese and chopped parsley.

HOMOUS ON THE CHEAP

1/2 can chick peas - rinsed
2-3 cloves garlic
2 Tbsps peanut butter
1 lemon
1 Tbsp sesame oil
3 Tbsps yoghurt

Blend all the above ingredients in a food processor or blender until smooth and thick. Dilute with a little water or more yoghurt if necessary. Serve in a bowl with pita bread.

PERUVIAN NOODLE EGGS

4 eggs
3 Tbsps grated parmesan cheese
2 Tbsps crushed saltine crackers
3 Tbsps milk
Fresh basil or 1/2 tsp dried basil
Salt & pepper
Butter

Whisk the eggs with the parmesan cheese, crackers, milk, basil, salt & pepper. Melt some butter in a frypan, put in 2 Tbsps of the mixture and tip around the pan. Turn it over when done and cook the other side. Remove to a plate and repeat until you have a few. Roll the omelettes up one by one and cut into noodles, about 1/4" wide. To cook, toss them in a frypan with 2 Tbsps butter and the chopped basil. Serve on a pool of tomato sauce and sprinkle with parmesan cheese.

BEER & CHEESE FONDUE

2-3 cloves garlic - finely chopped
2 Tbsps butter
2 Tbsps flour
1 bottle beer
2 1/2 cups grated cheddar cheese
1 tsp dried chillies
1 tsp dry mustard
1/2 tsp nutmeg - optional

Melt the butter in a saucepan and stir in the garlic. Add the flour and stir vigorously until smooth. Pour in the beer, stirring all the time, and bring to the boil. Add the grated cheese and seasonings. When it has all melted, turn the heat down very low and keep warm or pour into a fondue pot. Arrange some raw vegetables or chunks of good bread to dip into the fondue.

MAYONNAISE, (Three Colours)

Make three types of mayonnaise by mixing 2 Tbsps of mayonnaise with 1 tsp each of curry powder, tomato paste and the third one of curry powder AND tomato paste. Arrange the three different colours on a platter and scatter with cherry tomatoes. Halve the hard-boiled eggs and arrange on the mayonnaise. Garnish with chopped parsley.

BEANS TOSCANA

3/4 cup cannellini beans - rinsed and soaked overnight
2 Tbsps olive oil
2 Tbsps chopped parsley
1 onion - finely chopped
2 tomatoes - chopped
1/2 tsp salt
1 can tuna
2 cloves garlic - chopped
1 tsp oregano
1/2 lemon
Cherry tomatoes to garnish

Rinse and drain the beans. Place in a large saucepan with plenty of water and bring to the boil. Cover and simmer for about 45 minutes. Drain and place in a bowl. Add all the remaining ingredients, toss well and serve.

BEANS WITH SPICY SAUSAGE

Follow the recipe as above except replace the can of tuna with a chopped chorizo sausage and garnish with some diced red pepper.

DUXELLES

4 Tbsps butter
1 lb old mushrooms - chopped finely

1 onion - finely chopped
2 Tbsps parsley
1 Tbsp pepper
1 tsp thyme

Melt the butter in a frypan and add the onion. Stir well, with the heat up high, until they start to colour. Add the mushrooms, parsley and seasonings and allow to cook down, with the lid off, for 2-3 minutes, keeping the heat high. Freeze in ice-cube trays, covered with plastic and use when needed e.g. for mushroom omelettes.

EASY PASTA SAUCES

SPRINGTIME QUICKIE SAUCE

1 bunch green onions - chopped
1 tomato - chopped
1 Tbsp chopped parsley
Squeeze of lime juice
1/2 tsp salt
1 Tbsp olive oil

Blend all the above ingredients in a food processor or blender. Toss with some cooked pasta and dust with some grated parmesan cheese.

WINTER PESTO SAUCE

1 bunch cilantro
2-3 cloves garlic
2 Tbsps olive oil
2-3 Tbsps grated asiago cheese
2 Tbsps walnuts

Blend all the above ingredients in a food processor or blender, adding a little water if necessary. Toss with some cooked pasta and dust with some grated asiago cheese.

PUTTANESCA SAUCE

2 Tbsps olive oil
1 chopped onion
6 chopped tomatoes
2 cloves garlic - chopped
6 anchovy fillets
Bay leaf
1 Tbsp tomato paste
2 Tbsps water
Freshly ground pepper
1 Tbsp capers
2 Tbsps black olives
1 Tbsp vinegar

Heat the oil in a sauté pan and brown the onions. Stir in the anchovies and mash until they melt, add garlic, tomatoes, bay leaf, tomato paste and water, bring to a boil, put the lid on and simmer for 10 minutes. Finish the sauce by adding the capers, black olives, vinegar and pepper, stir to heat everything through and toss with the pasta.

CARBONARA SAUCE

3-4 slices bacon - chopped
1 egg
1 chopped onion
2 cloves garlic - chopped
Freshly ground pepper
1 tsp oregano
1 Tbsp chopped green onion
1/2 cup heavy cream

Fry the bacon in a frypan and pour off any excess fat. Stir in the onions and when lightly browned add the garlic, pepper, oregano and green onions. Beat the egg with a little water and pour into the sauce stirring quickly. Add the cream, heat through and serve with pasta.

WALNUT & HORSERADISH SAUCE

1/2 cup shelled walnuts
3/4 cup yoghurt
2 Tbsp horseradish
1/2 tsp salt
Pinch sugar
2 Tbsps grated parmesan cheese
2 cloves garlic

Blend all the ingredients in a food processor and serve with hot pasta or chicken.

SPICY SAUSAGE SAUCE

1 hot, spicy sausage (Italian, Hungarian, whatever) chopped
1 Tbsp olive oil
1 chopped onion
3-4 whole cloves garlic
1/2 cup red wine
1 tsp oregano
1 tsp tomato paste
1 Tbsp chopped parsley

Heat the olive oil in a frypan and brown the onions. Add the garlic, spicy sausage, red wine and oregano and stir well. Put the lid on and cook for about 5-8 minutes until the sauce is a rich, dark colour. Sprinkle with chopped parsley and serve with pasta.

PASTA WITH RED PEPPER, ANCHOVY & BLACK PEPPER SAUCE

2 red peppers, chopped
3-4 anchovies
2 cloves garlic, chopped
1 hot, red pepper
Freshly ground black pepper
2 Tbsps olive oil
Juice of 1/2 lemon
Chopped parsley

Heat the oil in a frypan and sauté the peppers, anchovies, garlic and black pepper until melted. Serve on hot pasta garnished with chopped parsley and some parmesan cheese.

PASTA WITH RASPBERRY SAUCE

Leftover cold pasta
1 Tbsp butter
4 Tbsps raspberry jam
1/2 tsp pepper
Juice of 1/2 lemon
1/3 cup sherry

Heat the butter, jam, lemon juice, sherry and pepper in a pan and when just boiling pour over the pasta. Decorate with orange slices.

SPICY TURKEY PASTA

1 Tbsp oil
1 chopped onion
1 Tbsp chopped parsley
Freshly ground pepper
Cooked turkey meat - cut into bite-sized pieces
1 tsp cayenne pepper
1/2 red bell pepper
2 Tbsps olives

Heat up the oil in a frypan and sauté the onions (if you have a leftover pickled onion, chop up and add!). When transparent, add the turkey meat, parsley, black pepper and cayenne. Stir well and when heated through, add the chopped red pepper and some olives. Heat any leftover pasta by steaming it in a strainer over boiling water until hot. Tip onto a plate and top with the spicy turkey.

CARROT FETTUCINE

1 lb/450g carrots, peeled
2 Tbsps oil
1/2 cup light cream
1/2 tsp salt
1 tsp pepper
1/2 tsp nutmeg

1/2 cup grated parmesan
Chopped parsley

With a peeler, take long strips off the carrots. Heat the oil in a frypan and toss the carrots, salt, pepper and nutmeg for about 1 minute over high heat. Add the cream and some chopped parsley and cook, stirring, until the liquid has reduced by half. Serve immediately sprinkled with parmesan cheese and chopped parsley.

AGLIO OLIO

2 Tbsps olive oil
6 to 8 cloves chopped garlic
Handful chopped parsley
1 can anchovies
Freshly ground pepper
1 tsp vinegar

Heat the oil in a frypan and stir all the ingredients in. Cook for about 5 minutes until the anchovies have melted and made a sauce. Toss with some cooked pasta, such as linguine or rotini and serve.

ALFREDO THE QUICK

1 Tbsp dijon or grainy mustard
1/2 cup cream
2 Tbsps grated cheddar cheese
2 Tbsps chopped green onions
1 Tbsp chopped parsley
Freshly ground pepper
Grated nutmeg

Put the mustard into a frypan and add the rest of the ingredients. Cook for a few minutes, stirring all the time, until it has made a sauce and toss with some cooked pasta. Serve.

QUICK MEAT SAUCE

1 1/2 lbs/750g ground beef
1 onion - chopped
1 Tbsp olive oil
2 cloves garlic - chopped
1 medium can tomatoes
1 tsp oregano
1/2 tsp salt
Juice of 1/2 lime or lemon
Handful of black olives

Brown the meat in a frypan over high heat and add the rest of the ingredients, except the olives. Stir well, adding some liquid if necessary, and cook for about 15-20 minutes. Before serving, stir in the black olives and toss with some cooked pasta.

PUMPKIN IN A PASTA NEST

1 lb/500g pumpkin
1 Tbsp butter
Salt & pepper
1 tsp dill
1 Tbsp chopped green onions
1/2 cup chopped walnuts, lightly sautéed
1/2 lb/250g spinach pasta or angel hair pasta
1 Tbsp olive oil
1 clove garlic, chopped

Cook the pumpkin, peel and mash with the butter, salt & pepper and dill. Mix with the walnuts and green onion. Cook and drain the pasta. Heat the oil in a frypan and sauté the garlic. Add the drained pasta and toss well. Serve on a platter with the pumpkin mixture in the middle. Garnish with more chopped walnuts and green onions.

SALADA DE ATUN

1 lb/500g green beans
4 hard-boiled eggs - chopped
Handful each of green and black olives
1 can tuna
2-3 Tbsps mayonnaise or yoghurt

Blanch the green beans in boiling water for 4 minutes. Strain and rinse under cold water. Put in a large salad bowl, add the eggs, olives and tuna. Spoon on the mayonnaise or yoghurt and toss well. Season with freshly ground pepper and serve with hot potatoes.

☛ HOT POTATOES

Boil potatoes until cooked. Drain and sprinkle with 2 tsps hot sauce, and 1-2 Tbsps olive oil. Serve with freshly ground black pepper and some salt.

BAKED GARLIC

1 head garlic
Olive oil
Red wine

Take a piece of foil and double it over. Place the unpeeled head of garlic in the middle and make a package, leaving the top open. Drizzle over some olive oil and wine and bake in a 300 F/150 C oven for 30-45 minutes. Serve as a side dish or peel the cloves and mash onto some bread.

AVOCADO GINAIGRETTE

Peel and slice 2 avocados and arrange on a plate. Pour 1" of oil into a small spice jar, add salt and pepper, the juice of 1/2 lemon, 1/2 tsp cayenne pepper and some gin (a third the amount of gin to oil). Put the lid on and shake well, add an egg yolk to make gin mayonnaise and shake well again. Pour over the avocados and serve.

SALSA CRUDO (Almost Uncooked Tomato Sauce For Pasta, Chicken, Fish Or Chips)

4 tomatoes, halved and seeded
1/4 cup chopped green onions
1/4 cup chopped cilantro or parsley
1 Tbsp basil or oregano
2 cloves chopped garlic
1 tsp chopped jalapeno peppers or 1/2 tsp chilli flakes or 1 tsp hot sauce
2 Tbsps olive oil
Juice of 1/2 lime or lemon
1 tsp salt
1 tsp sugar

Dice the tomatoes, mix all the ingredients in a bowl and allow to stand. Serve over hot spaghetti or chicken breast or fillets of fish or just with tortilla chips.

SALSA & CORN

Salsa crudo (see above)
1 can corn or 1 small packet frozen corn, or fresh corn kernels
1 tsp dill
Spicy sausage
1 can drained, white beans
2-3 Tbsps olive oil

Mix together the salsa crudo, corn, dill and chopped spicy sausage and toss with the white beans. Add the olive oil and allow to sit for 20 minutes. Serve as a salad.

LENTIL SALAD

1 cup lentils
1 clove garlic, chopped
3 cups water
Juice of 1/2 lemon
Zest of 1 lemon
4 Tbsps olive oil
1/2 tsp salt
1/2 tsp pepper
1 red pepper, diced
4 green onions, chopped
Chopped cilantro

Boil the lentils and water for 10 minutes until the lentils are cooked but not mushy. Drain well and whisk in the lemon juice and olive oil. Mix in the rest of the ingredients and garnish with chopped cilantro.

COOL SUMMER SAUCE

1 Tbsp chopped onion
1 Tbsp chopped parsley
2 Tbsps chopped cilantro
1/3 cup white wine
1/2 tsp salt.

Blend all the ingredients, adding more wine if necessary. Serve cold with chicken, fish, bread or vegetables. Add some chopped tomato and some paprika or hot pepper to the above to make a salsa.

BANANA & BACON ROLLS

2 peeled bananas
2 rashers bacon
2 slices of bread

Halve the banana crosswise. Halve the bacon rasher and wind round each half of banana. Fasten with toothpicks and broil for 8-10 mins. Serve on pieces of fried or toasted bread.

POTATO LATKES

1 medium potato
1/2 onion
1 tsp flour
Salt & pepper
1 Tbsp oil

Grate the onion on the coarse side of the grater, then grate the potato. Mix them both with the flour and salt & pepper. Heat the oil in a small frypan over medium heat and fry the latkes light brown on both sides. Serve with either apple sauce or sour cream or perhaps bacon. Kids like them with fried eggs.

TOMATADA

Small potatoes
2 Tbsps olive oil
1 tsp tomato paste
1/2 onion, chopped
2-3 cloves garlic, chopped
2 Tbsps white wine
Chopped parsley

Boil some small, unpeeled potatoes. Drain and dry well. Slice and fry them in the hot oil until golden brown each side. Stir in the tomato paste, chopped onion, garlic and wine. Stir well until everything is well coated and colourful, stir in chopped parsley and serve.

PAILLASSON DE POMMES DE TERRES (Straw Mat Of Potatoes)

4 medium-sized, floury potatoes
4 Tbsp butter or butter and oil
Salt & pepper

Grate the potatoes and rinse well in cold water. Drain and wrap in a tea towel to remove the moisture. Season with salt and pepper. Heat the fat and when smoking hot, press in the potatoes to make a 1/2" layer. Cook about 10 minutes to crisp the bottom and turn. Add more fat and cook for a further 5 minutes.

POTATOES STEAMED IN BUTTERMILK

1 lb/500g potatoes
2 cups buttermilk
Salt & pepper
1/2 cup oatmeal, optional

Heat the buttermilk in a saucepan and add the peeled potatoes. Sprinkle with salt and lots of pepper, cover and simmer until the potatoes are tender, about 15 minutes. Serve with a knob of butter and sprinkled with toasted oatmeal.

GALETTE POLONAISE

2 cups cooked, mashed potatoes
4 anchovy fillets
1 hard boiled egg
1 Tbsp flour
2 Tbsp chopped parsley
1/2 tsp pepper

Chop the egg, anchovies, parsley and pepper and mix well into the mashed potatoes. Add the flour and make into small cakes. Dust with a little more flour and fry over medium heat until both sides are golden. Serve with some chopped hard-boiled eggs.

PAN HAGGERTY

1 lb/500g potatoes (appx. 3 large potatoes) - thinly sliced
1 onion - thinly sliced (using serrated knife)
1/4 lb/125g grated cheese
2 Tbsp oil
Salt & pepper

Put the oil into a frypan and cover the bottom with an overlapping layer of potato slices. Top with a layer of onion rings and then a layer of grated cheese. Repeat layers until all the ingredients are used up finishing with a layer of potatoes. Season with salt and freshly ground pepper. Put the lid on and cook over medium heat for about 15 minutes. Remove lid, place plate on the pan and turn the Pan Haggerty over onto the plate. Slide it back into the pan, cook another 10 minutes, sprinkle with parsley and serve. Leftovers make good lunchboxes.

SPICY FRIED RICE WITH PINEAPPLE & COCONUT

2 Tbsps oil
1 1/2 cups cooked rice
1 onion, chopped
1 carrot, chopped
1 tomato, chopped
1/2 green pepper, chopped
1/2 cup pineapple, chopped
2 cloves garlic, chopped
2-3 fresh chillies, chopped
Grated coconut
Chopped green onions

Heat the oil in a frypan and cook the onion, carrot, green pepper, garlic, tomatoes and chillies. Stir well over high heat for 2-3 minutes and add the rice and pineapple. Cook for 5 minutes and serve garnished with grated coconut and chopped green onion.

MEGADARRA

1 1/2 cups lentils

4 cups water

2 onions, sliced

6 Tbsps olive oil

1 cup long grain rice cooked

Salt & pepper

Chopped green onions

Boil the lentils and water for 20-30 minutes. Fry the onions and black pepper in the hot oil in a frypan until browned. Remove at least half of them and fry the rest until very brown. Drain the lentils. Stir the rice into the almost cooked lentils and the light brown onions. Add salt and pepper and cook for further 10 minutes. Pour into a bowl and garnish with the dark brown onion rings. Garnish with chopped green onions.

QUINOA SALAD

1 cup quinoa

1 tsp salt

2 cups boiling water or stock

2-3 Tbsps olive oil

1/2 onion, chopped finely

1 cup crumbled feta cheese

1/2 cup chopped fresh mint leaves

Salt & pepper

Wash and drain the quinoa and put into a saucepan with 2 cups of salted boiling water. Reduce heat, cover and simmer until the liquid has absorbed, about 10 minutes. Fluff the quinoa with a fork and add the feta, onion, mint, olive oil, salt and pepper. Toss well and serve.

PERUVIAN POTATO SALAD

2lb/1Kg potatoes, boiled in their skins

6 hard boiled eggs

1 tomato, sliced

1/2 cucumber, chopped

Radishes, chopped

Make a dressing in the blender or food processor of:

2 Tbsps oil

1/4 cup milk

2 Tbsps peanuts or 2 Tbsps peanut butter

1/2 tsp cayenne pepper

2 Tbsps feta cheese

1/2 tsp ground black pepper

1/2 tsp salt

1 small bunch coriander leaves

Slice the potatoes thickly and lay them flat side down on a dish. Pour the dressing over and decorate with eggs and vegetables. Eat hot, cold or lukewarm.

AIOLI ONE

1 egg yolk
1/2 tsp salt
1 tsp mustard
3 cloves garlic, peeled
1 cup oil

Blend the egg yolk, salt, mustard and garlic in a blender or food processor until well mixed. Slowly add the oil until you have an emulsion. Serve with simple steamed potatoes and chopped parsley, with fried potatoes, with pasta, with chorizo sausage or with boiled eggs.

AIOLI TWO

6-8 cloves of garlic
1 egg
1 Tbsp chopped parsley
1 tsp dry mustard
1/2 tsp salt
Freshly ground pepper
1/2 cup olive oil

Blend all the above ingredients in a food processor or blender until thick and smooth. Squeeze in the juice of a lemon and blend further. Serve with some fish fillets that have been lightly floured and sautéed in 1 Tbsp oil and 1 Tbsp butter, salt and pepper and cooked for 8 minutes per 1" thickness. Decorate with sprigs of parsley.

AIOLI AMB FRUITA

1 ripe quince or 2 ripe apples or pears or 1 can pears
3-4 cloves garlic, peeled
1/2 tsp salt
3/4 cup olive oil
1 avocado
Juice of 1/2 lemon
Chopped parsley

If using fresh fruit, peel, core and cube the fruit and cook in water for about 5 minutes or until the fruit is soft. Drain and cool. Chop the garlic, salt and parsley and put in the food processor or blender. Peel the avocado and add along with the fruit and lemon juice. Sprinkle in the salt and pepper and blend until smooth. Slowly pour in the oil until the mixture is thick and smooth. Serve with chicken, pork, rabbit or chorizo sausage.

LEFTOVER BROCCOLI SAUCE

2 cups cooked broccoli
1/3 cup olive oil
1 Tbsp vinegar
Juice of 1 lemon
1/2 tsp dried basil or 2 Tbsps fresh basil
1/2 tsp powdered cumin or 1 tsp curry powder

Salt and pepper
1 Tbsp tomato paste
1 Tbsp yoghurt

Purée everything in a blender or food processor. Serve cold with cold chicken, or warm with pasta. As an alternative, add some more yoghurt to the sauce, blend and pour onto a plate. Arrange halved hard-boiled eggs around the sauce and serve.

CLAM CAKES

1 can clams, drained & chopped
2 cups grated potatoes
1/2 onion, grated
1 egg, beaten
1 Tbsp dried parsley
Salt & pepper
2 packets saltine crackers
Cornmeal or breadcrumbs
Oil

Mix together the clams, potatoes, onion, crackers, parsley, salt and pepper. Form into small cakes, dip into the beaten egg and then the cornmeal and fry in batches until brown.

RED FLANNEL HASH

4 slices bacon, chopped
1 onion, finely chopped
2 Tbsps oil
2 cups cooked, mashed potatoes
1 can beets, diced
1 can corned beef, flaked
6 green onions
2 Tbsps chopped parsley
2 Tbsps cream
Salt & pepper

Heat the oil in a frypan and sauté the bacon and onion until transparent. Remove and put into the food processor with the rest of the ingredients. Return the mixture to the hot pan, press down firmly and cook over high heat for 10-15 minutes. Turn out, upside-down, and serve garnished with white onion rings.

"SUPER" SAUCE

1/2 cup red wine
1 cup cranberries
1 pear, peeled, cored & sliced
1 apple, peeled, cored & sliced
Zest & juice of 1/2 orange
2 slices ginger, julienned
1/2 tsp pepper
1/2 tsp cayenne pepper
1/2 tsp salt
2-3 Tbsps brown sugar
Juice of 1/2 lemon

Heat the wine in a saucepan and tip in the cranberries. Add apple and pear slices and the orange zest. Stir well and add the rest of the ingredients. Allow to simmer for 5-10 minutes until the sauce has thickened. Serve hot or cold.

EXOTIC PILAF

3 Tbsps butter
1 cup almonds
1 cup dried prunes, chopped
1 cup dried apricots, chopped
1/2 cup dates, chopped
1/2 cup dried figs, chopped
1 cup of raisins
1/4 tsp ground cloves
1/2 tsp cinnamon
1 cup rice
1 cup water
1 1/2 cups white wine
1/2 tsp salt
1 Tbsp bitter
Juice of 1/2 lemon

Melt 1 Tbsp butter in a fry pan and add the rice. Stir until all the rice is covered with butter and pour in the water and 1 cup of white wine. Cover and simmer for 15-20 minutes. Meanwhile melt 3 Tbsps of butter in a large frypan and sauté the almonds. When browned, stir in the fruits and spices until well coloured and stir in 1/2 cup of white wine. Pile the rice onto a platter and pour the fruits over the top.

BREAD SAUCE

1 cup of milk
1/2 cup white breadcrumbs
1 onion, finely chopped
6 or 8 cloves
1 Tbsp of butter
1/2 tsp salt
1 tsp pepper

Melt the butter in a frypan and sauté the onions until transparent. Add the salt, pepper and cloves and pour in the milk. Stir and add the breadcrumbs. Simmer for 5 minutes, adding more milk if necessary to make a thicker sauce. Serve with chicken, turkey or ham.

ROMAN BREAD SALAD

1 white loaf bread
3 tsps vinegar
1 cup water
1 cup grated cheese

Remove crusts from the bread, slice and moisten with vinegar and water. Cover a shallow bowl with these pieces. Make a dressing of the following:

| 1 Tbsp honey |
| 1 Tbsp mint |
| 1 clove garlic, finely chopped |
| 1/2 cup olive oil |
| 1 Tbsp vinegar |
| 1/2 tsp salt |
| 2 tsps pepper |
| 2 Tbsps chopped parsley |
| Tomatoes |

Mix all the ingredients together and pour over the bread salad. Sprinkle with the grated cheese and garnish with sliced tomatoes. Serve chilled

MAINS

CHICKEN, HENS, TURKEY, ETC.

CHICKEN WITH SHERRY AND PEARS

1 chicken breast, diced
1 tsp cornstarch dissolved in 2 Tbsps sherry
1 tsp pepper
1 Tbsp olive oil
1 tsp butter
1 firm pear, peeled, quartered and sliced thick
Juice of 1/2 lemon
1/2 tsp salt
2 green onions, sliced thin

Mix the cornstarch, sherry and black pepper together and toss with the chicken. Heat oil and butter in a frypan and sauté the chicken over medium heat until browned. Add pear slices, green onions, sherry, lemon juice and salt and toss all together. Sprinkle with paprika and serve with noodles.

CHICKEN & ORANGES

1 chicken breast - skinned & halved
1 Tbsp butter
1 Tbsp oil
Ginger - finger length piece julienned
Freshly ground pepper
1 tsp thyme
2 oranges - peeled and segmented
1 small head broccoli - broken into florets
Mushrooms - half a dozen.

Heat up a frypan and add the oil and butter. Put in the ginger strips and then the chicken. When showing white round the edges turn the chicken over and add some pepper and the orange segments. Put in the whole mushrooms and the thyme, place the broccoli florets on top and sprinkle with salt. Cover and simmer for about 10 minutes.

BLACK & WHITE CHICKEN FINGERS

1 chicken breast - skinned & cut into long fingers
2 eggs
Black sesame seeds
White sesame seeds
Oil for frying - depth of oil to about 1/3 up the pan

Heat the oil in a pan with high sides (medium heat, 350 F/175 C). Separate the eggs and put the whites into a bowl. Dip the chicken fingers into the whites then dip one end into the white sesame seeds and the other end into the black sesame seeds. Drop the chicken into the hot oil. Turn over when browning and remove after about 5-8 minutes. (N.B. When deep frying, keep a lid handy to put on pan, in case of fire. A tight fitting lid will immediately extinguish burning oil).

CHICKEN TOVARICH

1 chicken breast
2 Tbsps oil
5-6 whole, unpeeled cloves garlic
1 medium onion - chopped
1 cup walnuts - roasted in the oven
Handful of dried apricots
1 cup cranberry juice
1 tomato - quartered
2 whole, hot, red peppers
1/2 glass red wine
1 cup chopped old mushrooms

Heat the oil in a frypan over high heat. Cut up the chicken breast into bite-sized pieces and flour them in a plastic bag. Put the pieces into the hot oil and brown. Add the chopped onion, garlic, walnuts, apricots, tomato, hot peppers and pour in the cranberry juice. Put the lid on and cook for about 10 minutes. Pour in 1/2 glass of red wine and the mushrooms. Cook for a further 5-10 minutes. Serve garnished with grapes and chopped parsley.

COQ AU VIN

2 Tbsps oil
1 tsp butter
10-12 chicken legs
6-7 whole garlic cloves
2 onions - coarsely chopped
3-4 slices bacon - chopped
3 anchovy fillets
1 carrot - chopped
1 Tbsp shredded orange zest
1 tsp thyme
2 tsps tomato paste
1 Tbsp brandy
1 1/2 cups red wine
1 Tbsp pearl onions
1 cup mushrooms
Broccoli florets

Heat the oil and butter in a large sauté pan. Flour the chicken legs in a plastic bag and brown them in the oil. Add the garlic and onions and stir well. Add the bacon, anchovies, carrot, orange zest, thyme and tomato paste, stir and cook with the lid on for 10-15 minutes. Pour in the brandy and red wine, add the pearl onions and mushrooms and lay the broccoli florets on top to steam. Cook for a further 10 minutes and serve with steamed potatoes.

STEAMED POTATOES

Cut up some potatoes and place in a steamer over 1/2" of boiling water. Put the lid on and steam for 15-20 minutes. Serve with chopped parsley and the Coq au Vin.

DRUNKEN CHICKEN

In a deep saucepan boil enough water to cover the chicken. Put half a dozen knives and forks inside the chicken and lower it into the pan of boiling water. Bring back to the boil and cook for 5 minutes. Turn off the heat, put the lid on and leave for 8 hours or overnight. Remove the chicken and take off the skin. Make a sauce by mixing 3-4 Tbsps soy sauce, 1 Tbsp vinegar or lemon juice, 1 tsp sugar, 1/2 tsp cayenne pepper and 2 Tbsps whiskey or brandy. Serve the chicken in pieces with the dipping sauce.

MOROCCAN CHICKEN

1 Tbsp butter
2 Tbsps currants
1 Tbsp sultanas
2 Tbsp toasted pine nuts
1/2 cup dried apricots
2 boneless chicken breasts
1/2 tsp cinnamon
1 tsp ground saffron
Freshly ground pepper
1 1/2 cups apple juice

Melt the butter in a large sauté pan. Stir in the currants, sultanas, pine nuts and apricots and when they've plumped up lay the chicken breasts in the bottom of the pan. Turn the chicken over when the underside is brown and add the saffron, pepper, cinnamon and apple juice. Cook for a further 6-8 minutes with the lid on. Add some chopped cilantro, cook for 1-2 minutes and serve on couscous with a side dish of yoghurt sauce.

✒ COUSCOUS

1 1/2 cups boiling water
1 cup couscous

Add the couscous to the boiling water and stir. Put the lid on, turn off the heat and cook for about 10-15 minutes.

✒ YOGHURT SAUCE

2-3 Tbsps yoghurt
1/2 cucumber - grated
Juice of 1/2 orange
Cayenne pepper

Stir the yoghurt, cucumber and orange juice together and sprinkle with a little cayenne pepper. Serve with Moroccan Chicken & Couscous.

CHICKEN THAI STYLE

1 can coconut milk - stirred
2 cloves garlic - finely chopped
1-2 slices ginger - julienned
6-8 whole dried chillies
1/2 onion - chopped
1 lime or lemon

1-2 chicken breasts - cut into bite-sized pieces
1 small bunch asparagus - cut diagonally

Heat 3-4 Tbsps coconut milk in a frypan. Add the garlic, ginger, chillies, onion and 1 Tbsp of shredded lime zest. Stir well and when the onion is transparent add the chicken pieces. Cook for 5-6 minutes, add the asparagus, put the lid on and cook for further 2 minutes. Squeeze the lime juice over and serve garnished with chopped cilantro.

PICCATA DI POLLO

1 boneless chicken breast
1/2 cup white wine
Juice of 1/2 lemon
1 Tbsp butter
1/2 tsp tarragon
Salt & pepper

Dust the chicken breast with flour, shaking off the excess. In a plastic bag lightly pound each half in a plastic bag until doubled in size. Melt the butter in a frypan over medium heat, lay in the chicken and cook for one minute or just until the edges turn white. Turn over and cook another minute on high heat. Pour in the white wine, sprinkle with salt, pepper and tarragon and cook for another minute. Squeeze in the lemon juice and serve, pouring the juices over the chicken and garnishing with lemon slices.

ARROZ CON POLLO

2 Tbsps olive oil
6 chicken legs
1 onion - coarsely chopped
1 cup rice
2 cups water, stock, beer or wine
6 cloves garlic - finely chopped
Few saffron threads - soaked in milk for 5 minutes
Freshly ground pepper
1 tsp tomato paste
1 tsp oregano
1/2 tsp hot sauce or to taste
6 whole mushrooms
6 whole cherry tomatoes
Chopped parsley

Heat up the olive oil in a large sauté pan and sear the outside of the chicken legs in the hot oil. Add the onions and cook for a couple of minutes. Stir in the rice, garlic and water, stock or wine. When well mixed, add the saffron and milk infusion, the tomato paste, oregano and hot sauce. Stir again and simmer for 20 minutes with the lid on over a medium heat. Five minutes before serving, add the mushrooms, tomatoes and chopped parsley, turn the heat up high, stir and serve.

CHICKEN & CASHEW NUT CURRY

1 chicken breast - skinned & cut into bite-sized pieces
2 Tbsps roasted cashews
3 Tbsps yoghurt
1 heaped tsp curry powder

1 Tbsp oil
1 chopped onion
1 clove garlic - chopped
Freshly ground pepper
1/2 lemon
2 slices fresh ginger
1/2 tsp dried chillies or to taste
2 Tbsps chopped green onions

Marinate the chicken pieces in the yoghurt and curry powder (overnight if you wish). Heat the oil in a frypan over medium heat and lay in the chicken pieces. When the outsides are well coloured stir in the onion, garlic, pepper, lemon juice, ginger and chillies, turn up the heat and cook for 5-10 minutes. Add the cashew nuts and chopped green onions, stir and cook for 5 minutes over medium heat. Serve.

CHICKEN & GREEN BEANS

1 chicken breast - cut into bite-sized pieces
2 Tbsps oil
2 handfuls green beans, cut bite-size
Salt & pepper
1 lemon
1 tsp sesame oil
Sesame seeds

Heat up the oil in a frypan over high heat and add the chicken pieces. Turn them over in the hot oil until the chicken turns white. Immediately add the green beans and stir well. Season with pepper and salt, put the lid on and simmer for 5 minutes. Squeeze in the lemon juice and add the sesame oil. Stir in well and serve sprinkled with sesame seeds.

HUNGARIAN STYLE CHICKEN LIVERS

2 Tbsps oil
2 Tbsps flour
1 lb/500g chicken livers
1 chopped onion
2 cloves garlic - chopped
1 tsp paprika
1 red pepper - diced
1 green pepper - diced
1/2 cup red wine
3-4 sliced mushrooms

Flour the chicken livers in a plastic bag. Heat the oil in a frypan and add the livers. When the outsides are brown and crisp, stir in the chopped onion, garlic and paprika. Cook for 2 minutes. Add the diced peppers and pour in the red wine. Cook for 6-8 minutes, adding the sliced mushrooms at the last minute. Sprinkle with chopped parsley and serve on noodles with grated cucumber.

GRATED CUCUMBER

1/2 cucumber
1 Tbsp sour cream
1 tsp dill

Grate the cucumber and mix with the sour cream and dill. Pour into a small bowl and serve with the Hungarian style chicken livers.

FRENCH STYLE CHICKEN LIVERS

1/2 lb/250g chicken livers
1 Tbsp grainy mustard
1 Tbsp soy sauce
2 Tbsps brandy
Green and black grapes

Heat up a saucepan and put the chicken livers into the hot, dry pan. Stir in the mustard, soy sauce and brandy, put the lid on and cook over a low heat for 2-3 minutes. Quickly add a good handful of green and black grapes, cook for 1 minute and serve on a cabbage or lettuce leaf.

DEVILLED CHICKEN

2 chicken breasts - cut into lengths
1 cup breadcrumbs
1 Tbsp dry mustard
1 tsp curry powder
1 tsp cayenne pepper
1/2 tsp salt
Freshly ground pepper
Melted butter

Heat up a frypan with 1 Tbsp oil or leave dry. Mix the breadcrumbs, mustard, curry powder, cayenne pepper, salt and pepper together and dip the chicken pieces into the melted butter and then the breadcrumb mixture. Fry in the hot pan turning over when the underside is crusty and brown. Serve with mint & coriander chutney.

🖈 MINT, CORIANDER & COCONUT CHUTNEY

3 slices fresh ginger
2 cloves garlic
Juice of a lemon
1 Tbsp chopped onion
2 Tbsps grated coconut
Freshly ground pepper
1 bunch fresh mint
1 bunch fresh coriander
1 Tbsp vinegar
Water

Blend in a blender or a food processor all the above ingredients together adding enough water to make a chutney. Serve in a small bowl with devilled chicken.

CHICKEN À LA KING

1 cooked chicken breast - cut into pieces
1 1/2 Tbsps butter
1 Tbsp flour

1/2 onion - finely chopped
1/2 tsp salt
Freshly ground pepper
1/2 cup sliced mushrooms
1 tsp tarragon
3 Tbsps yoghurt or cream
1/2 red pepper -diced
1 Tbsp chopped parsley

Melt the butter over medium heat and stir in the flour to make a roux. Gradually add enough water to make a thick sauce and stir in the onions until soft. Add the seasonings, chicken pieces and mushrooms and stir in the yoghurt or cream until the sauce is smooth. Sprinkle on the red pepper and parsley, heat through and serve.

CHICKEN & PEANUTS

2 Tbsps oil
1 chopped onion
4 whole garlic cloves - unpeeled
4-5 hot peppers
1 chicken breast - skinned & cut into bite size pieces
1 Tbsp soy sauce
1 Tbsp vinegar
1 tsp fresh ginger - chopped
1 clove garlic - chopped
1 Tbsp cornstarch
2 Tbsps peanuts

Marinate the chicken pieces in the soy sauce, vinegar, ginger, garlic and cornstarch. Heat the oil in a frypan over a high heat and fry the onions until lightly brown. Stir in the garlic cloves, hot peppers and peanuts. Add the chicken pieces, keeping the high heat, and cook for a few minutes. Pour in about 1/2 cup of water and cook for further 2 minutes. Stir well and serve with some chopped cilantro.

VELVET CHICKEN

1 chicken breast - skinned & cut into bite-sized pieces
3 tsps cornstarch
1 tsp salt
1 tsp pepper
1 Tbsp oil
2/3 cup stock
1/2 lb small mushrooms
1/4" piece of fresh ginger - chopped

Mix the chicken pieces in a bowl with 1 tsp cornstarch, 1 Tbsp oil, 1/2 tsp salt and 1/2 tsp pepper. Let sit. Pour the boiling stock over the mushrooms in another bowl and stir in 2 tsp cornstarch, 1/2 tsp salt and 1/2 tsp pepper. Quick fry the chicken, over high heat for 30 seconds then add the mushroom mixture and the ginger. Stir constantly until just done, no more than 5 minutes, over medium heat. Serve immediately.

CHICKEN STEW & DUMPLINGS

1 1/2 lbs/750g chicken wings - tips removed.

2 onions - coarsely chopped

1/2 lb small carrots

1 tsp thyme

1 cup red wine, or white wine, or apple juice

1 cup water

3 sticks celery - chopped

1/2 lb cherry tomatoes

Few pearl onions

Cut chicken wings at joints with a sharp knife. Heat a non-stick frypan over medium heat , no oil, and put the chicken wings in. When both sides are browned stir in the remaining ingredients and put the lid on. Cook for 15-20 minutes. Meanwhile make the dumplings.

✦ DUMPLINGS

1 cup flour

2 tsps baking powder

1 egg - beaten

1/2 cup milk

Mix the flour and baking powder in a bowl. Pour the milk into the beaten egg and add to the flour mixture. Mix to a stiffish and dry consistency, adding more milk if necessary. Put spoonfuls of the mixture into the stew leaving room for them to expand. It's important that they steam so replace the lid and leave untouched for 6-8 minutes. Serve the stew & dumplings with chopped parsley.

COQ AU BIÈRE

2 slices bacon - chopped

4 chicken thighs

3 carrots - chopped

1 onion - chopped

Bay leaf

1 tsp thyme

1 bottle beer

1/2 tsp salt

Freshly ground pepper

Sauté the bacon in a frypan over high heat and add the chicken thighs, skin side down. Turn over and when brown on both sides add the chopped carrot, onion, thyme and pepper and stir well. Pour in the beer, put the lid and simmer with the heat turned down for about 20 minutes. Add the salt towards the end of the cooking. Serve garnished with chopped parsley.

CHICKEN AND 40 CLOVES GARLIC

2 Tbsps oil

40 cloves garlic - unpeeled

1 chicken breast - with or without the bone and cut into bite-sized pieces

1/2 tsp salt

Freshly ground pepper
1/3 cup red wine

Heat the oil in a frypan over high heat and lay the 40 cloves of garlic in the bottom. Add the cut up chicken pieces and stir well. When browned add the salt, pepper and red wine, turn the heat down to medium low and simmer with the lid on for 15- 20 minutes. Discard any garlic skins and serve with chopped parsley.

EIGHT-LEGGED CHICKEN

Buy a chicken and 6 extra legs. Stitch extra legs onto the chicken using cotton thread. Stuff the chicken with some chopped lemons and a handful of garlic and rub all over with salt. Roast in a 400 F/220 C oven, basting every 15 minutes, for 20 minutes per pound. Serve to astounded guests!

CHICKEN & LAVENDER

1 chicken breast - skinned and deboned
1 Tbsp cream cheese
1 Tbsp chopped lavender leaves or flowers
Pinch of salt
Freshly ground pepper

Have the steamer ready and throw some extra lavender into the boiling water to perfume it. Flatten the chicken breast in a plastic bag by beating with a rolling pin or bottle of wine. Cut into 2" wide strips. Mix the lavender, cream cheese, salt and pepper and spread about 1 tsp on each strip, roll it up and push a toothpick through. Lay cabbage or lettuce leaves in the steamer (to stop the chicken sticking) and place the chicken rolls on top. Steam for 6-8 minutes and serve. If preferred, roll up a whole chicken breast and serve in slices. If you haven't got a steamer, then put half an inch (1 cm) water in a frypan, bring to a boil, wrap the chicken breasts in a cling wrap and cook with the lid on for 10 minutes.

CHICKEN, CELERY & CIDER

4 chicken thighs
2 sticks celery, sliced diagonally
1 clove garlic, crushed
1 onion, chopped coarsely
1 bay leaf
1 apple, peeled, cored and sliced
1 bottle cider
1 tsp sage
1/3 cup cream
Salt & pepper

Heat a dry frypan over high heat and place the chicken thighs in, skin side down. When browned on each side, add the onions, bay leaf and celery. Stir for a few minutes until coloured and add the apple, salt and pepper. Stir until well coated and pour in the cider. Keep the pan over a high heat and let the cider bubble. Sprinkle in the sage and cook 5 more minutes. Just before serving, stir in the cream.

CORN STIR-FRY

1 chicken breast, chopped
1/2 onion, chopped

3 slices ginger, chopped
1 red pepper, chopped
2 Tbsps chopped cilantro or parsley
1 small packet frozen green peas
1 can whole baby corns or frozen corn kernels
1 tsp cornstarch
1 Tbsp vegetable oil

Heat the oil over high heat and put in the chicken, onion, ginger and red pepper. Stir for 1-2 minutes and add the peas and corn. Cook for further 3-5 minutes and stir in the cornstarch and cilantro. Serve immediately.

FRANGO COM ERVILHAS   (Chicken And Peas)

2 Tbsps olive oil
1 Tbsp butter
1 onion, sliced
2 chicken breasts
1/2 red pepper, diced
1 slice of cooked ham, diced
1 glass white wine
1/2 glass port or sherry
1 packet frozen peas

Heat a frypan with the oil and brown the chicken breasts. Add the onions and stir. Add the ham, butter, port and wine, season with salt & pepper and cook 10 minutes more. Add the frozen peas and cook for 2 minutes, stir in the diced red pepper and serve.

WHISKEY MARMALADE CHICKEN

2 chicken breasts, cut into pieces
1/2 onion, finely chopped
1 Tbsp butter
1 Tbsp oil
1/2 tsp cayenne pepper
1/2 tsp fresh ground pepper
1/2 tsp salt
2 Tbsps whiskey
2 Tbsps orange marmalade
Juice of 1/2 orange or lemon

Heat the oil and butter in a frypan and sauté the chicken pieces until light brown each side. Add the onion, pepper and salt and cook for 2 minutes. Add the whiskey and flambé, then stir in the orange marmalade. Add the orange juice and cayenne pepper, stir well and serve.

FEGATINO DI POLLO CON L'UVA

1 lb/500g chicken livers
2 Tbsps butter
1 Tbsp oil
1 cup seedless grapes or sultanas
1/2 cup white wine

Salt & pepper
Fresh basil

Heat the butter and oil over medium heat (use a biggish pan to give things room to move in it) add chicken livers and stir gently to coat them all with butter. Add grapes or sultanas, sprinkle at least 1 tsp fresh ground pepper, add wine and turn livers gently until done, (no blood comes when pressed gently with the back of a fork). Sprinkle with salt and serve immediately. Garnish with fresh basil leaves.

PAPAYA, CHICKEN & GINGER

1 chicken breast, cubed
1 papaya, cubed and skins saved
3 slices of ginger, julienned
1 clove garlic, chopped
5-6 whole hot, red peppers
1 Tbsp olive oil
Salt & pepper
2 Tbsps rum
Juice of 1/2 lemon or lime

Marinate the chicken in the cut up papaya skins and oil for 15 minutes. The skins are a tenderizer, something called "papain" and they will tenderize the meat - they will also tenderize your skin! Remove the chicken from the marinade, heat up the frypan and quick fry the chicken pieces. Add the cubes of papaya, ginger, garlic and hot peppers and stir well for 1-2 minutes. Season with salt and pepper, pour in the rum and flambé. Finish the dish with a squeeze of lemon or lime juice.

CHICKEN & PEPPERS

1 chicken breast, cubed
2 slices ginger, julienned
2-3 hot, red peppers
1 yellow pepper, chopped
1 Tbsp olive oil
Salt & pepper

Heat the oil in a frypan and sauté the chicken pieces until brown. Add the ginger, hot peppers and salt & pepper. Stir well and add the yellow pepper. Cook for further 2 minutes and serve.

POLLO CON NARANJAS

1-2 boneless chicken breasts
1/2 tsp cinnamon
1/4 tsp ground cloves or 4-5 whole cloves
4-5 whole, unpeeled, garlic cloves
Salt & pepper
4 Tbsps olive oil
1 onion, finely chopped
3 Tbsps blanched almonds
1/4 cup raisins
Strained juice of 6 oranges or 1 cup frozen orange juice
1/2 cup sherry

Sprinkle the chicken breasts with the cinnamon, cloves, salt and pepper. Heat the oil and fry the chicken over high heat until brown . Add the onion, garlic cloves and almonds. Stir well and add the raisins, (whole cloves if you're using them) orange juice and sherry. Keep over high heat and cook for 5-10 minutes or until the chicken is done.

CHICKEN WITH TOMATOES & PEANUT SAUCE

2 chicken breasts, cut into pieces
1 Tbsp oil
1 onion, coarsely chopped
2 tomatoes, chopped into eighths
1 slice fresh ginger, julienned
2-3 Tbsps peanut sauce
Black & white sesame seeds

Dredge the chicken pieces in sesame seeds and sauté in the hot oil. Add the ginger and onion and stir well. When the chicken is browned, add the tomatoes and stir in the peanut sauce. Cook for a further 2 minutes and serve with chopped coriander leaves.

 # PEANUT SAUCE

6 Tbsps peanut butter
1 tsp chilli flakes
2 cloves garlic chopped fine
2 Tbsps sugar
1 can anchovy fillets or 1/2 tsp shrimp paste
1 small can coconut milk or grated coconut and water
Juice of a lemon
Salt to taste

Put everything in a food processor and blend. Add more coconut milk or water, if necessary, to make the sauce a smooth, pouring consistency.

CHICKEN AND ALMONDS

1 chicken breast, cubed
2 Tbsp oil
6 hot chilli peppers or 1/2 tsp chilli pepper flakes
1/2 medium onion, chopped coarse
1/4 cup blanched almonds
1 bunch cilantro, chopped coarse.

Heat the oil in a frypan and quick fry the chicken over high heat for 1 minute. Stir in the almonds and cook for another minute. Add chilli pepper and the onion and cook for 1 minute. Finally stir in the chopped cilantro, salt and pepper, stir well and serve immediately.

CHICKEN & WATERMELON

2 chicken breasts, cut into bite-sized pieces
2 Tbsps olive oil
1/4 onion, finely chopped
1 clove garlic, finely chopped

1 tsp curry powder
1 carrot, slivered or grated
1 tsp pepper
1/2 tsp salt
1 cup seeded, peeled and diced watermelon
1/2 tsp cinnamon
2-3 slices fresh ginger, chopped

Fry the chicken pieces in hot oil over medium heat. Add the garlic and ginger. Stir well and add the watermelon, cinnamon, curry powder, salt and pepper. Simmer for 5-8 minutes stirring occasionally. Toss in the carrot, stir and serve.

SAGE CHICKEN WINGS

12 chicken wings
1 Tbsp butter
1 Tbsp olive oil
4 bacon slices, chopped coarsely
1 cup dry white wine
1 tsp dried sage
2 Tbsps fresh sage leaves
1/2 tsp salt
1 Tbsp pepper

Remove tips from the chicken wings. Heat the butter and oil in a frypan over high heat and add the wings and bacon. Shake well and fry until the wings are brown on both sides. Add pepper, salt, sage and wine, cover and cook for 10-15 minutes. Serve with lemon-scented rice.

LEMON SCENTED RICE

1 cup long-grain rice
2 cups water
1 lemon
3 Tbsps butter
Salt

Bring water and salt to a boil. Add the rice and return to the boil. Cover, lower the heat and simmer for 20 minutes. Remove lid and stir in the butter and the grated rind and juice of the lemon.

CHICKEN INVOLTINI

2 boneless chicken breasts
2 oysters
1/2 tsp salt
1/2 tsp pepper
1 tsp thyme
1 Tbsp oil
1 Tbsp butter
Green onions
1/2 tsp dill

Pound the chicken breasts between floured, waxed paper until thin. Season with salt, pepper and thyme. Lay an oyster and green onion on the breast and roll up into a small parcel. Heat the oil and butter in a frypan and sauté for about 5 minutes or until the chicken is lightly browned and tender. Toss the carrot in with the chicken, dill and some more pepper and cook for 2 minutes. Serve immediately.

CHICKEN MOLE

Basic Sauce

2 Tbsps oil
2 onions - finely chopped
1 lb/500g tomatoes - chopped
2 Tbsps finely chopped parsley
2 hot peppers - finely chopped
1 Tbsp finely chopped cilantro
Freshly ground pepper
1/2 tsp sugar

Heat the oil in a large frypan and sauté the onions and tomatoes over a medium heat. Stir in the rest of the ingredients and cook for about 5-10 minutes. Then add :

3 chicken breasts - skinned and halved
A good handful of oregano
1/2 tsp cinnamon
1 tsp ground cumin
Bay leaf
2 pieces unsweetened chocolate - grated
Juice of 1/2 lime

Stir and allow to cook for a further 15-20 minutes. Serve garnished with chopped parsley or cilantro.

CORNISH GAME HENS SARDINIAN STYLE

2 Cornish game hens
2 Tbsps oil
2 onions - coarsely chopped
Freshly ground pepper
8 whole cloves garlic
1 medium can tomatoes
3 anchovy fillets
1/2 cup water
1 tsp thyme
1/3 cup red wine
1 Tbsp capers
2 Tbsps black olives

Heat the oil in a large sauté pan and brown the Cornish game hens on both sides. Add the onions, stir well and cook for 5 minutes. Add the pepper, garlic, tomatoes, anchovies and water, put the lid on and simmer for 10 minutes. Pour in the red wine, add the thyme and capers and cook for a further 5 minutes. Finally add the black olives for the last 10 minutes of cooking, stir all around and serve garnished with chopped parsley.

ROASTED CORNISH GAME HENS

Rub salt all over 2 Cornish game hens. Stuff the inside with some pearl onions, tuck the wings underneath and place on a rack in a 400 F/200 C oven for 30 minutes.

DRUNKEN DUCK WITH GIN

1 chopped onion

1 grated carrot

4 duck legs

Freshly ground pepper

5-6 cloves

1/4 cup gin

1 tsp rosemary

1 Tbsp chopped orange zest

Apple juice to cover

Bay leaf

Combine all the above ingredients in a casserole dish and bake, covered, in a 350 F/180 C oven for 1 1/2 hours.

DUCK BREASTS

Sprinkle the duck breasts, skin side up, with a generous amount of salt and pepper and leave for about an hour. Put into a dry frypan and sauté over a high heat, fat side down, until brown and crispy. Pour in a little wine, boil it, add 1 tsp vinegar, and drizzle over duck. Eat with red cabbage.

TURKEY & BLUEBERRIES

1 turkey breast

1 onion, chopped

2 Tbsps oil

1 cup mushrooms

1 cup fresh or frozen blueberries

1 tsp tarragon

1 glass red or white wine

Salt & pepper

Flatten the turkey breast by beating it between two pieces of floured, waxed paper. Heat the oil in a frypan and sauté the onions. Cut the turkey into pieces and lay in the pan. Brown on both sides and stir in the mushrooms, blueberries and tarragon. Cook for 2 minutes and pour in the wine. Add salt and pepper, stir well and serve.

SPATCHCOCKED GAME HENS & OLIVES

Usually done in a casserole for a long slow baking. You can do that too and you can also cook it in a cast iron pot in the ashes of a fire but right now we'll go over it the quick and easy way.

2 game hens

1 med chopped onion

2 cloves garlic chopped

2 Tbsp olive oil

Bay leaf

1/2 cup of water or wine
12 large black or green olives, pitted
1 Tbsp capers
1 tsp mustard
4 Tbsps brandy or whiskey

Cut the game hens down the backbone with scissors. Heat the oil in a frypan over high heat and sear the hens. Turn over, reduce the heat and add the onion, garlic and brandy. Blend the olives and capers and add to the pan with the wine, mustard and bay leaf. Cook for about 25-30 minutes.

STUFFED TURKEY ROLL

1 flattened turkey breast
1 bunch chopped parsley
1/2 cup chopped walnuts
1-2 cloves garlic, chopped
1/2 chopped onion
Juice of 1 lemon
1 tsp butter
1 egg to bind
Salt & pepper
1 Tbsp butter

Place the turkey breast between two pieces of waxed paper, which have been sprinkled with flour, and beat with a heavy bottle. Mix all the ingredients, except the turkey breast, and spread over the breast. Roll and skewer with wooden skewers. Melt the butter in a frypan and pour over the turkey roll. Roast in a 400F/200C oven for 30 minutes. Remove and slice.

TURKEY & AVOCADO GOUGÈRE

3 Tbsps flour
3 Tbsps butter
1/2 tsp salt
1/4 tsp cayenne pepper
1/4 cup milk & water
3 eggs, beaten
2 Tbsps grated cheddar cheese

Mix the flour, salt and cayenne pepper. Heat the butter and milk mixture and bring to a boil. Add the flour, remove from the heat and beat well until the mixture forms a ball. Cool and gradually beat in the eggs until smooth and shiny. Stir in the cheese and spoon the mixture around a baking dish. Bake for 15 minutes in a 400F/200C oven until risen and brown.

Leftover turkey, cubed
Leftover chestnut stuffing
Leftover bacon, chopped
1 avocado, chopped
1/2 onion, finely chopped
1 Tbsp butter
1/4 cup cream

Meanwhile sauté the onion in the melted butter. Add the turkey, stuffing, bacon and avocado and heat through. Pour in the cream, stir and pour into the middle of the cooked gougere. Serve.

TURKEY & MINT TAGINE

2 Tbsps olive oil
1 stick cinnamon
6 whole cardamom
10 whole cloves
3/4lb/375g turkey meat, cubed
2 cups yoghurt
1 cup chopped mint
2 Tbsps raisins
1 tsp ground cumin
1 Tbsp coriander seeds
1/2 tsp salt
1 tsp pepper

Heat the oil and sauté the cinnamon, cardamoms and cloves. Add the turkey cubes and brown. Add the rest of the ingredients, bring to a boil and cook until thickened. Sprinkle with icing sugar and cinnamon. Serve with couscous salad and chopped fresh mint.

⟁ COUSCOUS SALAD

2 cups cold, cooked couscous
2 tomatoes, chopped
1/2 cucumber, chopped
1/4 cup chopped coriander or parsley
1/4 cup chopped mint
1 clove garlic, finely chopped (optional)
1 chilli pepper, finely chopped
Juice of 1/2 lemon
1 bunch green onions, finely chopped
1/4 cup olive oil
1/2 tsp salt
1 tsp pepper

Mix all the above ingredients together and serve garnished with chopped parsley or mint and crisp lettuce leaves on the side to scoop it up with.

FISH ETC.

BOUILLABAISSE

2 Tbsps oil or butter
2 onions - chopped
1 medium can tomatoes
2 sticks celery - chopped diagonally
1 bunch parsley - chopped
3-4 cloves garlic - chopped
1/2 red pepper - coarsely chopped
1/2 green pepper - coarsely chopped

1 tsp tomato paste
2 hot peppers
1 bottle beer or some wine
Salt & pepper
2 fish fillets (halibut, snapper etc.) - cut in chunks
1 bunch cilantro
1 Tbsp scotch, grappa, rye ,calvados etc.
Few mussels, clams & prawns

Heat the oil or butter in a large sauté pan and fry the onions, tomatoes, garlic and tomato paste. Stir and allow to make a sauce. Add the celery, peppers, seasoning and beer or wine and cook for about 10 minutes. Put in the fish pieces. Cook for about 5 minutes. Add the chopped cilantro, scotch and a few mussels, clams and prawns or whatever you have got, turn down the heat and cook for a further 5 minutes or a bit more on a low heat until the clams open. Serve garnished with chopped parsley or cilantro.

SALMON & GINGER

1 salmon steak
1 tsp butter
2 slices ginger - chopped
1/2 tsp hot red pepper

Take some foil and fold the edges to form a tray. Place the salmon steak on the foil and sprinkle over the ginger and hot red pepper. Dot with butter and place in the toaster oven on high or broil for about 5 minutes.

GINGER & FISH

4 slices ginger - julienned
1 tsp butter
2 fillets of red snapper (or other white fish)
1 bunch asparagus - stringy ends removed
1/2 tsp salt

Melt the butter in a frypan over medium heat. Add the ginger and stir. Dust the fish fillets with a little flour, shaking off the excess and place in the pan. Turn over when the underside has sealed, add the asparagus, some more butter if needed and sprinkle over the salt. Cook the fish a total of 7-8 minutes per inch of thickness. Arrange on a plate with the asparagus.

SHIOYAKE

Sprinkle a little salt on a plate. Place some salmon fillets or other fish fillets, on the salt with the skin side down and allow to sit for at least 10 minutes. Put the fillets into a hot, dry pan with the skin side down and cook for about 5-10 minutes with the lid on. Serve garnished with lemon slices.

CALAMARI

Fresh, or recently defrosted squid - cleaned and cut into rings

Batter:
1 cup flour
1 egg
1/2 tsp salt

Freshly ground pepper

1 tsp oregano

1/2 cup beer

Mix the ingredients for the batter. Heat up some oil for deep-frying which should come about 1/3 the way up a high-sided pan. Dip the squid rings into the batter and then into the hot oil and cook for only 1-2 minutes. DO NOT OVERCOOK and DO NOT OVERFILL THE PAN. Remove and serve with lemon wedges, chopped parsley and tzatziki.(see page 16) If you don't want to make the batter, simply dip the squid rings into seasoned flour.

SQUID THAI STYLE

1 Tbsp oil

1/2 lb/250g ground pork

7-8 hot chilli peppers - whole

2-3 cloves chopped garlic

2 slices chopped ginger

1 doz squid - cleaned

1 bunch chopped mint

1 lime

Cilantro

Heat the oil in a frypan, add the pork and chilli peppers and stirring energetically with a fork, cook over a high heat for about 5-10 minutes. Stir in the garlic and ginger. When the pork is cooked, cut open the squid tubes, lay them flat and score into a diamond pattern with a sharp knife, Cut into bite sized pieces. Add the squid to the pork mixture, stir, add the mint and lime juice. Cook for 2 minutes and serve on a plate garnished with the chopped cilantro.

SQUID IN RED WINE

1 Tbsp olive oil

2 onions - thinly sliced

7-8 whole squid - cleaned

2-3 cloves chopped garlic

Freshly ground pepper

1 tsp oregano

1/2 cup red wine

Heat the oil in a frypan and add the onion rings. When transparent put in the squid (and heads if liked) and stir. Add the garlic, pepper, oregano and wine and cook for 5 minutes. Take out the squid and boil the wine down to a thickish sauce. Arrange on a bed of rice and garnish with chopped parsley.

KEDGEREE

1 tsp butter

1 cup cold, cooked rice

1 fillet cooked, smoked fish

4 hard-boiled eggs - chopped

1 bunch green onions - chopped

1 tsp curry powder

2 Tbsps light cream

2 Tbsps chopped parsley

Freshly ground pepper

Melt the butter in a frypan and stir in the rice. Flake the fish into the rice and add the curry powder and pepper. Stir well. Add the green onions, chopped eggs and cream. Heat through thoroughly and serve with chopped parsley.

SNAPPER VERA CRUZ

2 Tbsps oil

1 1/2lbs/750g red snapper - cut into 3 pieces

1 onion - chopped

2-3 cloves garlic - chopped

1 Tbsp tomato paste

1 can tomatoes - or equivalent fresh

1 Tbsp capers

1 lemon or lime

1 Tbsp vinegar

Handful black olives

Heat the oil in a frypan and stir in the onions, garlic, tomato paste and tomatoes. Stir until the onions are cooked and the sauce is a rich, red colour. Add the capers, lemon juice, vinegar and black olives, make a hole in the sauce and place in the fish fillets. Put the lid on and cook for 8 minutes per 1" thickness of the fish. Garnish with chopped cilantro.

STUFFED PAPAYA

1 papaya

Cottage cheese

Fresh peeled shrimp

Fresh prawn tails

Freshly ground pepper

Cilantro

Halve the papaya and remove the seeds. Scoop out the flesh and chop. Half fill the shells with cottage cheese and arrange the chopped flesh around it. Top with a mound of fresh, peeled shrimp and decorate with a few fresh prawn tails. Grind some pepper over the top and garnish with cilantro. Serve on crushed ice.

SALMON FISHCAKES

1 can salmon - drained

1 onion - finely chopped

Leftover mashed potatoes

Freshly ground pepper

1 Tbsp chopped parsley

2 eggs

1 Tbsp oil

Breadcrumbs or cornmeal

Put equal parts of mashed potato and the salmon into a large bowl, add the chopped onion, pepper, parsley and 1 egg and mix together well with a fork. Beat up the other egg in a bowl and dip spoonfuls of the fish mixture into the egg and then into the breadcrumbs or cornmeal. Heat up the oil in a frypan, put in the fishcakes and pat down. Cook over medium heat until brown and crusty on both sides and serve with tomato ketchup or salsa.

 ## SALSA

1/2 onion - finely chopped
1/2 green pepper - finely chopped
1/2 red pepper - finely chopped
1 Tbsp oil
1/2 tsp cayenne pepper
Salt & pepper

Mix all the above ingredients and toss well in a small bowl.

SALMON & CABBAGE KOREAN STYLE

2 Tbsps oil
1 onion - coarsely chopped
3-4 slices ginger - chopped
1 cabbage - core removed and coarsely chopped
1/2 tsp salt
Freshly ground pepper
1 can salmon
1 Tbsp sesame oil

Heat up the oil in a frypan over high heat and stir in the ginger. Add the onions, then the cabbage. Toss the cabbage around to coat it with oil and sprinkle with salt and freshly ground pepper. When the cabbage has cooked down, add the can of salmon and stir. Cook for a few minutes. DO NOT OVERCOOK. Turn out onto a plate and sprinkle with sesame oil.

ASPARAGUS & SALMON SALAD

1 bunch asparagus - stringy ends removed
3-4 slices ginger - julienned
1/2 tsp salt
1 can salmon- drained
1/2 cup water
2 Tbsps oil

Heat the water and oil in a frypan, add the asparagus and sprinkle with salt. Add the ginger and cook. with lid on for 4 minutes. Remove the asparagus from the pan and arrange it on a plate around the canned salmon .

Dressing:

2 Tbsps yoghurt
1 tsp dill
Juice of 1/2 lemon
1 tsp sesame oil

Stir all the ingredients together and pour over salad.

SKATE AU BEURRE NOIR

1 Tbsp oil	
Skate wing cut into large pieces along the line of the ribs.	
Flour	
1 Tbsp butter	
1 Tbsp vinegar	
1 Tbsp capers	

Heat the oil in a frypan. Dust the skate with flour and shake off any excess. Lay the pieces into the hot oil and cook, turning once, allowing 8 minutes per 1" of thickness. Melt the butter in a small frypan and when it just starts to brown add the vinegar, bring the heat up and add the capers. Serve with the skate.

CARIBBEAN SHRIMP

1 onion - chopped
2 Tbsp butter
1 red pepper - chopped
1 cup cooked rice
1/2 tsp chilli powder
1/2 lb/250g peeled, fresh shrimp
1/2 tsp salt
2 bananas
Garlic - optional
1/2 cup cream

Melt the butter in a frypan over a medium heat and sauté the onions. Stir in the red pepper and cooked rice, making sure the rice is well mixed in. Add the chilli powder, salt, garlic, if using and the shrimp. Peel and slice the bananas, stir in and finally pour in the cream. Serve on lettuce leaves garnished with lemon twists.

TROPICAL SUNRISE FISH

1 Tbsp butter
2 fillets of white fish - e.g. snapper or cod
3 green onions - halved and cut lengthwise
1/2 tsp salt
1-2 Tbsps grated coconut
2 bananas
1/2 tsp cinnamon

Melt the butter in a frypan over medium heat and when hot, lay in the fish fillets. Turn over when the underside is browned and toss in the green onions, salt and coconut. Add the chopped bananas and cinnamon, heat through and serve. The fish will cook for 8 minutes per 1" of thickness.

SALMON TRICOLEUR

1 salmon steak
1 small lump of butter
1 small packet frozen peas
1/2 cup frozen orange juice
1 tsp dill or mint

Heat a dry, non-stick frypan over high heat and place the salmon fillet in, skin side down. Leave to sear until the top colours. Add the peas, butter, orange juice and dill and cook for a few minutes (7 minutes per 1" thickness of fish).

BOSTON COD

1 cod fillet, cut into 3 pieces
1 Tbsp oil
3-4 tomatoes
1/2 red onion, chopped
1 tsp tomato paste
1 tsp oregano
1 tsp pepper
1/2 tsp salt
1/2 tsp sugar
1 Tbsp red wine vinegar
Cornmeal
Milk/cream

Heat the oil in a frypan. Dip the fish into some milk or cream, dredge in cornmeal and sauté about 7 minutes per 1" thickness. Remove the fish to a warm plate and add the onion and chopped tomatoes to the frypan. Stir in the tomato paste and sprinkle with oregano, salt, pepper and sugar. Add the vinegar and stir well to make a sauce. Serve with the fish.

CUCUMBER & KIPPER STIRFRY

1 lb/500g smoked kipper fillets or 1 can kippers (smoked herring)
1/2 cucumber
1 bunch green onions
1 block firm tofu, cut into 1/8ths
1 Tbsp oil
1 Tbsp soy sauce
2 tsp lemon juice
2 tsp poppy seeds
Black pepper

Skin the kippers and cut diagonally into thin slices. Cut cucumber into finger length strips and do the same with the onions. Heat the oil, add the onions and cook for 2-3 minutes. Add the kipper, tofu and cucumber and cook for 1-2 minutes. Mix in the soy, lemon juice, pepper and poppy seeds. Stir for 2-3 minutes and serve. If you don't want to put kippers in, then stir in 1 Tbsp sesame oil for the last 30 seconds.

SPICY MINT NOODLES WITH SHRIMP

1 medium onion, chopped
3 Tbsps vegetable oil
5 or 6 hot chillies or 1 tsp chilli flakes
2 cloves garlic, chopped fine
1/2 lb ramen noodles
1 chopped tomato
2 Tbsps soy sauce
1 cup soaked, dried shrimp
1 cup mint leaves or 2 tsps dried mint
1 lime

Put the dried shrimp into a bowl and cover with boiling water. Allow to sit for about 10-20 minutes. Heat the oil in a frypan and sauté the onions and chilli peppers for 2 minutes. Add the chopped tomato, garlic and ramen noodles. Sauté for 2 minutes. Add 1 cup of the shrimp soaking water, cover and simmer for another 2 minutes. Stir in the soy sauce, mint leaves and the soaked shrimp. Toss all together, cook for 2 minutes and serve with lime wedges and mint leaves.

SPINACH PANCAKES WITH CANNED SALMON

2 Tbsp butter
4 Tbsp flour
1 1/4 cups milk
3 eggs
1 pkg frozen spinach, thawed, squeezed dry & chopped
1/2 cup grated cheddar cheese
1 can of salmon, drained and flaked
2 Tbsps mayonnaise
1 tsp curry powder

Melt butter, stir in the flour and cook, stirring vigorously, for 1 minute. Slowly add milk and cook until the sauce thickens (3 minutes). Take off heat, and beat in the chopped spinach, grated cheese and 3 eggs. Pour into a frypan in a thin layer and cook over medium heat until the top is just dry . Remove to a plate, and cook another. Mix the salmon, mayonnaise and curry powder together and spread this filling on the pancake. Stack the other pancake on top and continue layering them. Allow to sit and slice carefully.

OYSTER STEW

1 onion, finely chopped
1 Tbsp butter
1 1/2 cups milk
1/2 cup cream
1 Tbsp white wine
6-8 large oysters
3 slices fresh ginger
1 tsp orange zest, julienned
1/2 tsp salt
Pepper
Chopped parsley
Few drops of tabasco
Chopped green onion

Sauté the onion in butter until softened and add the oysters. Add the milk, ginger, salt, pepper, tabasco & orange zest. Cook slowly until the oysters float. Pour in the cream, sprinkle with parsley and chopped green onion and serve.

CRAB CAKES

1 can/1/2 cup crabmeat
1 small onion, chopped fine
1 tsp dry mustard
1/2 tsp cayenne pepper or hot sauce
2 Tbsp mayonnaise
1 egg beaten with 2 Tbsp whipping cream

1/4 cup of cracker crumbs

2 Tbsp vegetable oil

Extra breadcrumbs

Mix all the ingredients together, except the oil and breadcrumbs, and form into cakes. Coat with breadcrumbs and fry in the oil in a medium, hot frypan. Serve with remoulade sauce :

✒ REMOULADE SAUCE

1 small red pepper, diced

1 cup mayonnaise

1 small lemon, zest of

2 Tbsp chopped jalapenos or 1/2 tsp hot sauce

1 Tbsp horseradish

1 Tbsp capers

1/4 cup chopped, fresh parsley

Whizz all together in a food processor and sprinkle with chopped parsley. Actually, whizz up anything with mayonnaise, anything to make it spicy.

GRILLED FISH WITH PAPAYA BUTTER

Cook fish on a ridged grill pan for 5-7 minutes or pan fry.

1 ripe papaya (peeled)

1/2 cup unsalted butter

3 Tbsps white wine

2 tsp lime juice

2 tsp orange juice

Blend all the above ingredients in a food processor and chill. Serve with grilled fish.

FISH WITH PEANUT SAUCE

2 fillets fresh white fish (cod, snapper, halibut)

1 Tbsp black pepper

1/2 tsp salt

1 Tbsp vinegar or tamarind juice

Small bunch coriander leaves

2 Tbsps oil

1 lemon

Rub the fish with a lemon half and sprinkle to cover with black pepper. Heat the oil in a frypan and fry fish both sides until 3/4 cooked (5 minutes per inch of thickness). Add vinegar and 3 Tbsps of peanut sauce to the pan. Spoon over the fish and cook 2 minutes more. Serve with chopped coriander leaves and lemon wedges.

✒ PEANUT SAUCE

6 Tbsps peanut butter

1 tsp chilli flakes

2 cloves garlic chopped fine

2 Tbsps sugar

1 can anchovy fillets or 1/2 tsp shrimp paste

1 small can coconut milk or grated coconut and water

Juice of a lemon

Salt to taste

Put everything in a food processor and blend. Add more coconut milk or water, if necessary, to make the sauce a smooth, pouring consistency.

SALMON EN CROUTE

4 slices bread

1 Tbsp butter

1 can salmon

1 Tbsp grated cheddar cheese

1 egg

1 Tbsp milk

1 tsp paprika

1/2 tsp dill

Salt & pepper

Oil

Butter each slice of bread. Drain the salmon and mash with the cheese, pepper and dill. Spread this mixture over 2 of the slices of bread. Top with the other half and press firmly together. Beat the egg, milk, salt and paprika and dip the sandwiches in the mixture. Fry them in hot oil until brown on each side. Drain and serve with chopped green onions.

MEDITERRANEAN FISH STEW

4 fish fillets, cut into bite-sized pieces

2 Tbsps olive oil

5 cloves garlic, whole

1 red onion, chopped

1 can tomatoes

2 Tbsps chopped parsley

1/2 tsp hot pepper flakes

1/2 cup dry white wine

1 tsp thyme

Salt & pepper

Heat the oil in a frypan over high heat and sauté the onion, hot peppers and garlic. Stir in the tomatoes, thyme, salt and pepper and bring to the boil. Simmer for 5 minutes. Add the chopped parsley, wine and lemon juice and for the last 1-2 minutes of cooking, add the fish pieces. Serve immediately.

HALIBUT & BEETROOT

2 halibut steaks

1 Tbsp butter

1-2 cups milk

1 tsp black peppercorns

1/2 tsp salt

1 beetroot

1 apple

Juice of 1/2 lemon

Melt the butter in a frypan and put in the halibut steaks. Pour in the milk, add the salt and peppercorns and gently poach the halibut steaks until tender or about 5-8 minutes. Grate or thinly pare the beetroot and apple and arrange on a plate, squeeze over the lemon juice and place the halibut on top. Garnish with chopped parsley and lemon wedges.

TROUT IN CHERMOULA

1 onion, finely chopped

4 cloves garlic, finely chopped

1/2 tsp ground cumin

1/2 tsp paprika

1/2 tsp cayenne pepper

1/2 tsp powdered saffron

1/2 cup chopped coriander

1/2 cup olive oil

Juice of a lemon

1/2 tsp salt

2 trout, cleaned & dry

1 Tbsp oil

Marinate the trout in the above ingredients for an hour, rubbing the mixture well in. Remove from the marinade, dredge in flour and fry in the hot oil for 5 minutes per finger thickness. Stir in the marinade and serve hot with chopped coriander leaves.

TROUT IN OATMEAL

2 fresh trout, cleaned

2 Tbsps oil

Oatmeal (not instant) or flour

Heat the oil in a frypan. Dry the trout and dredge either in oatmeal or flour. Lay in the hot pan and cook for 7 minutes per inch thickness of fish. Serve with lemon wedges.

PORK, SAUSAGES, ETC.

PORK CHOPS & APPLES

1 Tbsp oil

1 onion - roughly chopped

2 pork chops

1 apple - peeled

2 Tbsps apple juice

2 cloves garlic - optional

2 Tbsps cream

1 tsp thyme

Heat frypan over med/high heat. When hot add the oil, then the pork chops. Cut apples into rings and remove cores. Turn heat down to medium, add the chopped onion, stir and arrange the pork on top of the onions. Add the apple slices, toss them a bit to coat with the pan juices, add the apple juice. Put lid on and cook for about 10 minutes until pork is cooked. Rub the thyme between your fingers and add to the pan, turn up the heat and cook for further 1 minute. Add the cream, bring up to the boil, remove from heat and serve with parsley.

CABBAGE & GARLIC SAUSAGE

1 green cabbage - cut into 1" slices
1 garlic sausage
2 Tbsps oil
1 onion - coarsely chopped
1/2 tsp salt
1 Tbsp pepper
1 tsp caraway seeds
1/2 cup water

Heat the oil in a large frypan and put in the chopped onion and cabbage. Turn the cabbage well in the pan to get it "blessed" with the hot oil. Cut the garlic sausage into 1" slices or smaller pieces if preferred and add to the cabbage. Sprinkle with salt, pepper, caraway seeds and pour in the water. Put the lid on and cook for about 10-15 minutes.

BLACK HAT CHILLI

2 Tbsps oil
1 1/2lbs/750g pork cubes
2 medium onions - coarsely chopped
1 tsp chilli powder or to taste
1 large can tomatoes
4 dried black mushrooms - soaked in water, wine or beer for 10 minutes
1 grated carrot
2 Tbsps molasses
1/2 bottle beer
1 bunch chopped, fresh cilantro
1 tsp salt
1 fresh corn on the cob
1 Tbsp vinegar
1 Tbsp chopped green onion
1 oz. bourbon

Heat the oil in a large saucepan and brown the meat. Add the chopped onions and the rest of the ingredients leaving the cilantro, salt and green onion until the last 3-4 minutes of cooking. If the chilli is too hot smooth it out with some chopped lettuce leaves. Serve with guacamole, sour cream, grated cheese and taco chips.

MINCED PORK CUTLETS

1 1/2lb/750g ground pork
6 Tbsps breadcrumbs
1 tsp paprika
2 eggs
2 Tbsps tomato ketchup
1 tsp Worcestershire sauce
1 Tbsp chopped parsley
2 Tbsps oil

Mix all the above ingredients in a bowl, form into shapes and roll in breadcrumbs. Heat up another Tbsp oil in a frypan and cook for about 10 minutes until well done. Remove to a plate. Add some tomato ketchup and the juice of a lemon to the pan, stir and pour over the cutlets.

PIZZAIOLA

4 quick- fry (thin cut) pork chops
1 Tbsp olive oil
2 chopped onions
1 tsp tomato paste
2 cloves garlic - chopped
1/2 lb cherry tomatoes
1 Tbsp capers
Bay leaf
1 1/2 cups red wine
2 Tbsps chopped parsley
1 tsp oregano

Marinate the pork chops in milk for a few minutes. Meanwhile heat the oil in a sauté pan and stir in the onions, tomato paste and garlic. Add the cherry tomatoes, capers, bay leaf, red wine and oregano and simmer with the lid on until the tomatoes have melted down into a sauce. Remove the pork chops from the milk and quickly seal each side in a dry frypan with the heat up high. Transfer the chops to the sauté pan and bury them in the sauce. Add 2 Tbsps chopped parsley and simmer for 5 minutes.

PATATAS VAREAS

1 spicy chorizo sausage - cubed
2 potatoes - cubed
2 Tbsps olive oil
2 anchovy fillets
3 whole garlic cloves
1 tsp tomato paste

Heat the oil in a frypan and stir in the potatoes over a high heat. When they're brown and crispy add the anchovies, garlic and tomato paste. Stir well until the anchovies and tomato have melted and add the chorizo sausage. Stir once, turn the heat down and cook for 15-20 minutes with the lid on. Serve with chopped parsley.

HAM & CIDER SAUCE

Quickly fry 2 thick slices of cooked ham and serve with cider sauce:

CIDER SAUCE

1/4 cup brown sugar
1 1/2 Tbsps cornstarch
1 cup cider
1/4 cup raisins
1/4 tsp salt
8 whole cloves
1 stick cinnamon or 1/2 tsp cinnamon
1 Tbsp butter

Melt the butter in a saucepan and stir in the sugar, raisins, cider, salt, cloves and cinnamon. Cook for 5 minutes. Mix the cornstarch and a little cider together in a small bowl and add to the sauce. Stir well until it thickens, strain and serve with ham steaks.

LA ROUZOLE

1/3 lb/170g ham - chopped
1/3 lb/170g ground pork
4 cloves garlic - chopped
2 Tbsps chopped parsley
1 tsp mint
3 eggs

Mix all the above ingredients in a bowl and add:

1/2 cup fresh breadcrumbs
1/2 cup flour
Salt & pepper

Make sure everything is well mixed, let stand for 20 minutes to an hour and make it into a thick pancake. Heat 2 Tbsps oil in a frypan over a high heat and press down into the pan. Flip over when the underside is done. Both sides should be dark brown and crusty and sound hollow when tapped. Eat as is, or add it to any soup in small pieces. Or let it cool and take it to lunch the next day, or keep it wrapped until the next time you make a soup.

TOFU AND PORK STIR-FRY

1 packet fried tofu
1/2lb/250g ground pork
2 green onions, chopped
1/2 red pepper, chopped
3-4 slices fresh ginger, julienned
Handful of mushrooms, sliced or dried chinese mushrooms, soaked
1/2 tsp hot, red pepper
1 tsp cornstarch or arrowroot
1 tsp vinegar
1 Tbsp oil

Cut the tofu into large cubes. Heat the oil in a frypan and sauté the ginger. Add the ground pork and stir for 3 minutes, until starting to brown. Stir in the green onions, mushrooms, pepper and hot pepper. Mix the cornstarch with the vinegar in a small bowl and stir into the mixture. Cook for another minute and serve immediately.

If you add some sesame oil, it becomes Korean-style; some oyster sauce Cantonese-style; a lot more red pepper its sort of Szechuan-style...but right now its ours: yours and mine !

PORK STIFADO

4 boneless pork chops
2 Tbsps olive oil
2 onions - sliced into thick rings
8 whole garlic cloves
Orange zest - julienned

1 stick celery - chopped
8 cloves
1/2 tsp cinnamon
1 can tomatoes or 8 fresh tomatoes
Bay leaf
1 tsp oregano
Chopped parsley

Heat the oil in a large sauté pan and brown the pork chops on both sides. Turn up high and add the onions, garlic, celery, orange zest, cloves, cinnamon and tomatoes. Stir well, add a little water or stock if necessary and simmer with the lid on for 10 minutes. Turn the heat down, add a bay leaf and the oregano and simmer for a further 15 minutes. Serve garnished with chopped parsley.

MEATBALLS

1 chopped onion
2 cloves garlic
2 Tbsps ground pork
1 cup cooked rice
Freshly ground pepper
1 tsp oregano
Lemon zest - grated or chopped fine.
2 eggs

Mix all the above ingredients well and form into small balls. Heat 2 Tbsps olive oil in a frypan and fry the balls in batches until brown and crispy. Serve with a yoghurt sauce made by mixing 3 Tbsps yoghurt, 1 Tbsp chopped green onions and 1 tsp oregano.

PORK & CELERY STEW

1 1/2 lbs/750g pork shoulder - cubed
2 Tbsps oil
1 onion - cut into wedges
1/2 head celery - chopped
1/2 head fennel - chopped
Freshly ground pepper
1 tsp fennel seeds
6 whole cloves garlic
1 cup white wine
1 tsp cloves
2 Tbsps yoghurt
1 lemon

Heat the oil in a large frypan and fry the pork until lightly browned. Stir in the onion and when it starts to brown, add the celery, fennel, garlic and seasonings. Pour in the white wine, put the lid on and simmer over a medium heat for 20-25 minutes. Just before serving, stir in the yoghurt and lemon juice, heat through and serve garnished with chopped parsley.

PORK, TERRIBLY SOPHISTICATED

1 lb/500g pork tenderloin - sliced crosswise

2 Tbsps flour
1 Tbsp oil
2 Tbsps cooked spinach
2-3 Tbsps cream
1/2 tsp grated nutmeg
1/3 cup white wine

Put the flour in a plastic bag and flatten each piece of pork in it by beating with a rolling pin or bottle of wine. Heat the oil in a frypan over a high heat and fry the pork pieces until brown on each side. Meanwhile heat the spinach, cream, nutmeg and wine in a saucepan and blend into a purée. Pour this sauce onto a plate and top with the pork medaillons.

PORK & CLAMS

1 1/2 lbs/750g lean, boneless pork or shoulder - cubed
4-5 cloves garlic - chopped
2 cups dry white wine
2 Tbsps olive oil
1 hot pepper - whole
2 onions - chopped
2 cans clams
Freshly ground pepper
4 medium tomatoes - chopped
2 cloves

Marinate the pork cubes in the white wine and garlic for 1 hour or overnight if wished. Heat up the oil in a frypan over high heat. Remove the pork cubes from the marinade and sauté quickly. Add the hot pepper, bay leaf, onion, tomatoes, cloves and a generous amount of freshly ground pepper. Stir well, turn the heat down and simmer for 10-15 minutes with the lid on. Pour in 1 can of clam juice, the rest of the marinade and 2 cans of drained clams, stir and cook for further 5 minutes. Just before serving add some chopped cilantro.

PORK CHOPS WITH WALNUTS

4 pork chops
2 Tbsps olive oil
1/2 onion, thickly sliced
1/2 onion, thinly sliced
1/2 cup toasted walnuts
1/2 cup red wine
1 tsp thyme
1/2 tsp salt
1 tsp pepper
1 cauliflower, broken into florets
1 tsp grated nutmeg
1 red pepper, chopped

Heat a large sauté pan, pour in the oil and sear the chops on each side. Quickly brown the thin onion rings in the pan, remove and keep warm. Add the thick onion rings and stir in the salt, pepper and thyme. Pour in the wine, stir in the walnuts and simmer for 5-8 minutes, adding more wine if necessary. Put a steamer in the middle of the pan and add the cauliflower florets. Cover and cook for 5 minutes. Add the red pepper to the pork chops for the last few minutes of cooking. Remove the cauliflower florets and sprinkle with grated nutmeg. Serve the pork chops on a platter garnished with the thin onion rings and the cauliflower florets arranged around the outside.

LENTILS & SAUSAGE (Lentejas Con Morcilla)

1 cup brown lentils, washed
1 bay leaf
6 Tbsps olive oil
3 whole cloves garlic, peeled
1 onion, finely chopped
1 tsp flour
1/2 tsp paprika
1/2 cup chopped spicy sausage or bacon
Salt & pepper

Put the lentils in a saucepan and cover with 2 1/2 cups of cold water, add the bay leaf, bring to the boil, cover and simmer for 25 minutes. Drain and put aside. Heat the oil in a frypan and sauté the onion and sausage until light brown. Add the garlic cloves, paprika and flour and stir well. Toss in the lentils, salt and pepper and stir for 2-3 minutes, adding extra lentil liquid if necessary. Serve.

VEAL HONGROISE

1 lb/500g stewing veal or pork
1 Tbsp butter
1/2 red onion, chopped
1/2 cup slice mushrooms
1 tsp paprika
1/2 tsp dry mustard
1/2 tsp nutmeg
2 Tbsps whipping cream

Slice the veal or pork thin, melt the butter in a frypan and brown the meat. Add the chopped onion, mushrooms, mustard and nutmeg and stir well. Add the paprika and cook for 3-5 minutes. Stir in the cream and serve over wide noodles.

FRIED SAUSAGES IN CRANBERRY JUICE

1/2 lb/250g chipolata sausages (pork)
1/2 cup cranberry juice
1 tsp thyme or rosemary
1 tsp pepper
1/2 tsp salt
1/2 cup frozen cranberries

Heat a dry frypan and put in the chipolatas. Sauté until lightly browned. Add the cranberry juice, thyme, salt & pepper and cook until the sauce has reduced. Add the frozen cranberries, cook for 2 more minutes and serve on braised lettuce leaves.

☛ BRAISED LETTUCE LEAVES

Tear up lettuce leaves into large shreds. Heat 1-2 Tbsps olive oil in a frypan and sauté the leaves, turning them well. Sprinkle with a little salt and pepper and serve with sausages.

GREEN BEAN STIR-FRY

1/2 lb/250g ground pork/beef
1/2 lb/250g long chinese beans (or runner beans)
1 onion, coarsely chopped
1 clove garlic, finely chopped
1 tsp sugar
1/2 tsp cornstarch
1 Tbsp vinegar
Hot red pepper
Salt & pepper
1 tsp sesame oil
1 Tbsp soy sauce

Heat the oil in a frypan over a high heat and brown the pork. Add the garlic, onion and ginger and stir well. Mix the cornstarch with vinegar and stir in together with the sesame oil and soy sauce. Cut up the beans into finger-length pieces and add. Sprinkle with a little salt to help keep the green colour of the beans and toss everything together well. Serve immediately.

STEAMED GROUND PORK - CHINESE STYLE

1/2 lb/250g ground pork
1/2 tsp 5-spice powder or allspice
2 tbsps sherry
2 Tbsps soya sauce
1/2 tsp pepper
1 cup rice
2 cups water

Put the rice and water on to cook. Mix together all the rest of the ingredients and pat into a large cake. Place this carefully on top of the cooking rice, cover and steam until the rice has cooked and absorbed all the water. Remove the meat. Tip the rice onto a plate and decorate with chopped cilantro, place the meat cake on top and serve.

SPINACH PANCAKES KOREAN STYLE

1/4 lb/125g ground pork
2 Tbsp oil
1 clove garlic, chopped
2 bunches green onions
1/2 tsp cayenne pepper

Fry the pork, garlic, cayenne pepper and one bunch of finely chopped, green onions until the meat is browned. Cut the other bunch of green onions across into thirds. Push the pork mixture to one side, lay in the green onions across the pan and spoon the pork mixture back on top. Pour over some spinach pancake mixture (see Spinach Pancakes with Canned Salmon page 72) and jiggle to level it. Fry until the spinach mixture has set. Mix equal parts of soy sauce and rice vinegar in a small bowl to make a dipping sauce and serve with the pancake.

ISLAND PORK

1 pork tenderloin, sliced crosswise
2 cups chopped pineapple

1 heaped tsp dijon mustard

1/2 cup coconut milk

2 Tbsps rum

1 Tbsp oil

Heat the oil in a frypan over high heat and lay in the pork slices. Brown the pork and add the pineapple, dijon mustard and rum, stir in the coconut milk and add salt and pepper. Serve with chopped cilantro or parsley.

ITALIAN SAUSAGE WITH CARROT, FENNEL & CABBAGE

3/4lb/350g Italian sausage (or ordinary)

1/2 cup red wine

1 onion, chopped

2 carrots, sliced diagonally

1/2 small cabbage, chopped

1/2 fennel bulb, sliced or 3 stalks celery & 1/2 tsp fennel seeds

1 clove garlic, chopped

1/2 tsp salt

1 tsp pepper

1/2 tsp oregano

Chop up the sausage and cook in a frypan until browned. Add the wine and garlic and boil until reduced. Remove to a plate. In the same pan, adding 1 Tbsp oil if needed, sauté the onion and carrot to the pan and brown. Stir in the cabbage, fennel, salt and pepper and toss. Put the sausage back in, add more wine if needed, and 1/2 tsp oregano. Toss until the cabbage is slightly wilted and everything is well mixed and serve. Garnish with fennel leaves.

SPICY PORK, COCONUT & BLACK PEPPER RICE

3/4 lb/350g pork tenderloin, sliced

3 Tbsps oil

6 shallots, peeled & whole

8 green onions, trimmed to 6"

6 chilli peppers

1 can coconut milk

1/2 cup water

3 Tbsps fish sauce or 1 can anchovies

2 Tbsps black pepper

Coriander

Rice

Heat the oil over high heat and sauté the green onions until brown. Remove, add the peppers and shallots and sauté until brown. Add the pork slices and sauté for 2-3 minutes, stirring well. Stir in the fish sauce or anchovies, turn the heat down and add the coconut milk and black pepper. Pour the pork over cooked rice and arrange the green onions around. Sprinkle with more black pepper and coriander leaves and have extra in small bowls on the side.

BEEF

WHITE HAT CHILLI

2 Tbsps oil
1 1/2lbs/750g ground beef
2 medium onions - coarsely chopped
4 whole, peeled cloves garlic
1 tsp hot sauce or to taste
1 1/2lbs fresh, roma tomatoes
1/2 lb whole, white mushrooms
1 bay leaf
1 bottle cider
1 tsp thyme
1 medium can red kidney beans
2 Tbsps liquid honey
1 tsp salt
1 bunch chopped fresh mint
1 tsp sesame oil
2 Tbsps brandy

Heat the oil in a large saucepan and brown the meat. Add the onions and the rest of the ingredients leaving the fresh mint, salt and sesame oil until the last 3-4 minutes of cooking. Serve with guacamole, sour cream, grated cheese and taco chips.

GINGER WITH BEEF & ORANGE PEEL

1 small piece flank steak
1 tsp cornstarch
1 Tbsp soy sauce
Freshly ground pepper
2 Tbsps oil
2 slices ginger - julienned
2 cloves garlic - coarsely chopped
Strips of orange peel
1 tsp dried chillies or cayenne pepper
1/2 lb cherry tomatoes

Mix the cornstarch, soy sauce, pepper and 1 Tbsp oil in a bowl. Slice the flank steak across the grain into very thin slices and chop into three. Put the beef into the bowl and stir with the marinade. Heat up 1 Tbsp oil in a frypan, add the ginger strips and garlic and stir. Add the beef, orange strips, the hot chillies and finally the cherry tomatoes. Stir over high heat for 5-8 minutes and serve, garnished with parsley, on rice.

SHEPHERD'S PIE

1 lb/500g ground beef
Leftover mashed potatoes
2 Tbsps oil
2 onions - finely chopped
1 tsp rosemary - chopped

1 carrot - grated
Freshly ground pepper
2 Tbsps Worcestershire sauce
1 egg

Heat the oil in a frypan. Put in the onions, rosemary, carrot and freshly ground pepper and stir well. Add the ground beef and stir until the meat changes colour. Tip into a baking dish, sprinkle with the Worcestershire sauce and mash down. Mound some mashed potatoes on top and make a pattern with a fork. Lightly beat the egg and brush over the top with a pastry brush. Bake in a 425 F/225 C oven for 30 minutes. Serve with fried tomatoes and mushy peas (see below).

CEVAPCICI

1/2 lb/250g ground beef
3-4 Tbsps finely chopped onion
1 egg
Freshly ground pepper
1 Tbsp chopped parsley
1 tsp oregano
1 tsp paprika
2 Tbsps oil
1 tomato - chopped
1/3 bottle beer
1/2 tsp salt

Heat the oil in a frypan. Mix the remaining ingredients in a bowl and stir well. Form into finger length sausages and put into the frypan. Turn over when browned and turn the heat down. Push to one side and add the chopped tomato, beer and salt and cook for a few minutes more.

FAGGOTS

1/2 lb/250g liver
1/2 lb/250g ground beef
1/2 cup chopped mushrooms
1 tsp thyme
1/2 finely chopped onion
Freshly ground pepper

Drop the liver into boiling water for 1 minute then grind, with the rest of the ingredients, in a food processor until smooth. Heat the oil in a frypan and fry small spoonfuls of the mixture until dark, nutty and brown. Serve with mushy peas and fried tomatoes.

🡒 MUSHY PEAS

Put some frozen or canned peas in a saucepan with a little water. Sprinkle 1 tsp flour over the top and bring to a boil. Turn the heat down and simmer with the lid on 15 - 20 minutes.

🡒 FRIED TOMATOES

Slice a large tomato and dip each slice in flour, shaking off the excess. Fry in a little oil or butter until golden and crusty. Season and garnish with chopped parsley. Very good with red tomatoes, but wonderful with green ones in the fall.

BREADED VEAL (OR TURKEY OR CHICKEN) SCALLOPS & ANCHOVY BUTTER

4 veal, chicken or turkey scallops
2-4 anchovies
6 Tbsps butter
Flour
Salt & pepper
2 eggs, beaten
1 cup breadcrumbs

Mix the anchovies into the butter and chill in a small dish or form into pats, wrap in waxed paper and put in the fridge. Season the flour with salt & pepper. Beat the scallops in a plastic bag until flattened thin and dredge them in the flour. Dip them in beaten egg and breadcrumbs, melt 1 Tbsp butter or oil in a frypan and sauté for 5 minutes each side over high heat. Serve with the anchovy butter.

STIR-FRIED BEEF WITH LEEKS

1 Tbsp soy sauce
1 Tbsp fish sauce (or 1-2 anchovies)
1 tsp cornstarch
1/2lb/250g sirloin steak, sliced thin
2 Tbsps oil
3 leeks, chopped
6 outside leaves of a romaine lettuce, shredded
1 Tbsp chopped cilantro/parsley
1 tsp chilli flakes
1 Tbsp vinegar
1 Tbsp sugar
2 Tbsps soy sauce

Marinate the beef in the soy sauce, fish sauce, cornstarch, chilli flakes, vinegar and sugar. Heat the oil in a frypan over high heat and sauté the beef for 3-4 minutes. Add the leeks and lettuce and toss well, put the lid on and simmer for 1-2 minutes. Sprinkle with cilantro and serve.

CORNED BEEF HASH

1 can corned beef
2 potatoes - grated
1 medium onion chopped fairly coarse
1 Tbsp freshly ground pepper
1 egg
1 Tbsp oil
1 tsp dry mustard
1 tsp thyme or oregano - optional

Chop up the corned beef and place in a large bowl. Add the grated potatoes, pepper and egg and mix up thoroughly with hands. Heat up the oil in a frypan and when hot put in the corned beef hash and pat down with a fork into a cake. Sprinkle the mustard on top, turn down to a medium heat and cover. When brown underneath, put a plate on top and flip over the cake onto the plate. Slide back into the pan and cook the other side. Leave off the lid to ensure it keeps crispy. When cooked, slide onto platter and decorate.

LAMB

VENISON (But Really Lamb)

Lamb chops
1 Tbsp chopped parsley
1 Tbsp chopped garlic
1 Tbsp chopped orange & lemon zest
1 Tbsp pepper
1 tsp cloves
1 tsp rosemary
1 cup cranberry juice
1/2 cup red wine
1 Tbsp oil

Marinate the lamb chops in all the above ingredients for about an hour. Sauté in a dry frypan over high heat until done to your liking. Serve with red cabbage.

LAMB CHOPS SOFIA

6 loin or rib chops
2 Tbsps oil
2 Tbsps chopped celery
1 onion - chopped
4 cloves garlic - chopped
1 cup chopped tomatoes
1 Tbsp chopped red pepper
1 Tbsp chopped green pepper
1/3 cup rice
2/3 cup water
1 tsp oregano
1/4 lb mushrooms - whole
Juice of 1/2 lemon
1/2 tsp salt

Heat up the oil in a large frypan and immediately put in the lamb chops. When browned on both sides, add the celery, onion, garlic, tomatoes and peppers and stir well. Add the rice, water, oregano, mushrooms and lemon juice. Stir again, turn the heat down to very low and simmer for 15-20 minutes with the lid on. Add the salt at the last minute and serve.

QUICK LAMB CURRY

2 Tbsps oil
1 onion - thinly sliced
1/2 lb/250g lamb tenderloin - cut into bite-sized pieces
5 whole garlic cloves
2-3 Tbsps sultanas
1 apple - chopped
2 tsps curry powder
Juice of a lemon
1 cup water
2 Tbsps grated coconut

Heat up the oil in a large frypan and sauté the onion rings over a high heat. Add the lamb, garlic, sultanas, apple, curry powder and lemon juice and stir well until lightly browned. Pour in the water and grated coconut, turn down the heat and simmer for about 15 minutes with the lid on. Serve on rice and garnish with lime wedges and chopped cilantro with chutney.

✒ CHUTNEY

1 Tbsp chopped onion
1 Tbsp grated coconut
Juice of 1/2 lemon
1 tsp sugar

Blend all the above ingredients in a blender adding a little water. Mix in 1 Tbsp grated carrot and 1 Tbsp chopped parsley and serve with the lamb curry.

GREEK LAMB SOUBISE

Small, boned loin of lamb
2 sticks celery, chopped
2 carrots, chopped
1 onion, chopped
1 Tbsp oil
1/2 cup breadcrumbs
1/2 cup chopped apricots
2 Tbsps white wine
Salt & pepper
1 tsp sage

Lay a few apricots down the middle of the lamb, roll and tie up with string. Heat 1 tsp of olive oil in a hot frypan and brown the meat. Remove and keep warm. Heat 1 Tbsp olive oil in the pan and fry the celery, carrots, onion and breadcrumbs, stirring well. When slightly coloured, add the chopped apricots, salt, pepper, sage and wine. Mix well and lay the meat on top. Cover and simmer for 10 minutes.

LAMB, GIN & CIDER

1 lb boned & cubed leg of lamb
1 Tbsp oil
3 carrots, sliced diagonally
1 onion, finely chopped
4 slices fresh ginger, chopped
1 tsp thyme
Salt & pepper
1/2 bottle cider
1 Tbsp apple cider vinegar
1/4 cup gin

Heat the oil in a frypan and sear the lamb cubes. Lay the carrot slices on the bottom of the pan and brown on both sides. Stir in the onion, ginger, pepper, salt and thyme and cook for 2-3 minutes. Pour in the cider, stir in the vinegar and finally add the gin. Mix well and cook for about 3 minutes.

LAMB & PUMPKIN STEW SERVED IN A PUMPKIN

1 lb/500g pumpkin, peeled, seeded and cut into cubes
1/2 lb/250g cubed leg of lamb
2 Tbsps olive oil
2 cloves garlic, chopped
1 tsp sugar
1/2 cup water
1 Tbsp chopped parsley
1 Tbsp chopped cilantro
1 tomato, chopped
1 tsp ground ginger
Juice of 1/2 lemon
1 Tbsp sugar
1/4 tsp cayenne pepper
1 Tbsp ground cumin
Salt & pepper

Heat the oil in a frypan and brown the meat. Add the onion, cayenne pepper, sugar and garlic and stir well. Add the rest of the ingredients, except the cumin, cover and simmer for 5 minutes. Pour into a hollowed out pumpkin and put in a 400F/200C oven for 30 minutes. Garnish with cumin and some more chopped cilantro.

ROAST RACK OF LAMB

1 rack of lamb
2 Tbsps brown sugar
1 tsp dry mustard or 1 Tbsp dijon mustard
1 tsp pepper
1/2 tsp salt
2 Tbsps oil
Zest of 1/2 lemon
Fresh rosemary or 1 tsp dried

Mix together the sugar, mustard, pepper, salt and oil and rub all over the lamb. Lay in a baking dish and sprinkle with the lemon zest and rosemary. Bake in a 425F/220C oven for 25-30 minutes. Serve with roast potatoes.

ROAST POTATOES

Take some small potatoes, cut a slice off one end and stand up. Cut into slices being careful not to cut right through, and leaving the potato whole. Sprinkle with some parmesan cheese and drizzle with oil. Roast in the oven around the rack of lamb.

RACK OF LAMB

2 racks of lamb
1 can anchovies
3-4 cloves garlic
1 Tbsp brown sugar
1 Tbsp soy sauce

Score the lamb with a diamond pattern. Blend the rest of the ingredients in a blender to a smooth paste and rub all over the lamb. Place on a rack in a preheated 400 F/200 C oven surrounded by some cherry tomatoes and bake for 15-20 minutes. Serve the racks "cathedral-style", upright with the bones interlocking, with the cherry tomatoes and some trenchers of baked bread.

VENISON OR LAMB EN CROUTE

3/4lb/350g puff pastry

4 lamb loin chops (preferably boneless)

1/2 cup dried apricots, chopped

3 slices ginger, julienned

1 Tbsp oil

Fresh rosemary sprigs or dried rosemary

1/2 tsp salt

1 tsp pepper

Roll out the pastry and cut into 4 rectangles. Sear the chops in hot oil and place one in the middle of each rectangle. Put some chopped apricots on top of each one and a sprig of rosemary. Sprinkle with salt and pepper and bring the pastry edges together to seal into a parcel. Brush the tops with a little milk and beaten egg yolk and bake for 20 minutes in a 400F/200C oven.

EGGS N' STUFF

SPANISH OMELETTE

1 Tbsp olive oil

1/2 onion - finely chopped

2 Tbsp canned tomatoes

1 Tbsp chopped green pepper

2 cloves chopped garlic

1 tsp thyme

Heat a small frypan and sauté the onions in the hot oil. Add the tomatoes, pepper, garlic and thyme and cook for 5-10 minutes.

3 eggs

1 1/2 eggshells water (1/2 eggshell water per egg)

1/2 tsp salt

1 tsp butter

Break the eggs into a bowl, add the water and salt and beat with a fork. Heat up a frypan on high and when hot enough that water flicked on to it bubbles, melt the butter and pour in the eggs. Keeping the heat high, let sit for a minute and when the rim starts turning white, shake the pan and stir with the fork. Allow the bottom to set and pour the filling across the omelette. Pick up the pan from underneath and slide onto a plate flipping the top half over. Garnish with parsley and serve immediately.

HUEVOS RANCHEROS

3-4 Tbsps basic Chicken Mole sauce (see page 62)

1 Tbsp oregano

| 1/2 tsp ground cumin |
| 1 Tbsp chopped parsley |
| 2 eggs |
| 1/2 red pepper |
| Freshly ground pepper |

Dilute the sauce with a little water if necessary and heat in a frypan. Add the oregano, cumin and parsley and stir. Break the eggs into a small bowl, make a hole in the middle of the sauce and slide gently in. Add some red pepper strips and freshly ground pepper and cook until the eggs are done. Slide out onto a plate to serve.

FRIED EGG AND POTATO SLICES

| 1-2 cooked potatoes |
| 1 Tbsp oil |
| 1 tsp caraway seeds |
| 1/2 red pepper diced |
| 1 Tbsp chopped parsley |
| 2 eggs |
| 1/2 salt |
| Freshly ground pepper |

Heat the oil in a frypan and put in the caraway seeds. Cut the potatoes into 1/4" slices and lay them in a circle around the outside of the pan. Turn them over when browned and break the eggs in the middle. Sprinkle the red pepper over the potatoes and add salt & pepper. Tip onto a plate when cooked and garnish with parsley.

POOR MAN'S SAUSAGES

| Stale bread |
| Milk |
| 1 egg, beaten with 1 Tbsp pepper |
| Flour |
| 2 Tbsps butter |

Cut the bread into fingers, dip in some milk and let drain. Dip in the beaten egg, dredge in flour and fry in butter. Pile into a pyramid and serve as a side dish or with a dip.

⬈ THREE DIPS

| Yoghurt |
| 1 Tbsp tomato paste |
| 2 Tbsps chopped parsley |
| 1 Tbsp curry powder |

Put some yoghurt in each of three bowls. Stir the tomato paste into one, the parsley into another and the curry powder into the third. Serve with the poor man's sausages.

FACTORY WORKERS' BREAKFAST

| 2 Tbsps oil |
| 1/2 onion, chopped |
| 3 wieners, chopped |

2 Tbsps sauerkraut
1 tsp pepper
1 tsp caraway
1 potato, diced
4 eggs

Heat the oil in a frypan and sauté the onion, wieners, sauerkraut and potato. Stir well and add the caraway seeds and pepper. Beat the eggs together with 1/2 eggshell of water and when the potato and onion have started to brown, pour the egg mixture over the top. Cook until the egg has set and turn out onto a plate. Garnish with chopped parsley or green onion.

OEUFS FLORENTINE

1 packet frozen spinach - thawed
1 tsp butter
1/2 onion - finely chopped
Freshly ground pepper
1/2 tsp salt
2 eggs
1 tsp vinegar

Melt the butter in a frypan and sauté the onions. Add the spinach, pepper and salt. Bring a saucepan of water to the boil, add 1/2 tsp salt and 1 tsp vinegar. Break the eggs onto a saucer. Stir the water round and gently slide the eggs into the pan, allow to poach for 5 minutes or until the yolks are just setting. Turn out the spinach onto a plate and make a nest. Using a slotted spoon carefully remove the poached eggs and lay on the spinach. Break the yolks and sprinkle with some grated nutmeg.

POTATOES, HORSERADISH & EGGS

Mash some cooked potatoes and mix in:

2 Tbsps cream
1 Tbsp grainy mustard
1 Tbsp horseradish sauce
Handful of chopped parsley
Salt & pepper
4 eggs

Put the mixture into a dish, make four holes with the back of a spoon and break an egg into each one. Put in a 350F/180C oven and cook for 20-25 minutes.

ZUCCHINI OMELETTE WITH CROUTONS

2 slices white bread, trimmed & diced
1 clove garlic
1 Tbsp olive oil
1 small zucchini, grated
3 eggs
1/2 eggshell of water
Salt & pepper
2 Tbsps grated parmesan cheese
1 Tbsp butter

Sauté bread cubes and garlic in the oil until crisp and golden. In a small bowl, beat the eggs, water, salt & pepper and stir in the grated zucchini and parmesan cheese. Melt the butter in a frypan and add the egg and zucchini mixture. When the bottom is set, fill the middle with the croutons, slide the omelette out onto a plate and flip over with the croutons inside. Serve sprinkled with some more parmesan cheese.

TORTILLA ESPANOLE (Spanish Potato Omelette)

2 potatoes, cubed
1 onion, chopped
2 cloves garlic, chopped
2 Tbsps olive oil
4 eggs
Chopped parsley
1/2 tsp cayenne pepper
1 tsp thyme
1/2 tsp salt
1 tsp pepper

Heat the oil in a frypan and sauté the potatoes until slightly softened. Add the onion, stir until transparent and add the garlic. Beat the eggs and the rest of the ingredients and pour over the potatoes. Cook until set and then flip over and brown the other side. Serve sprinkled with some chopped parsley.

RICE PANCAKES

2 cups cold, cooked rice
3 eggs
2 Tbsps sugar
1 tsp butter

Stir the rice, eggs and sugar together. Melt the butter in a small frypan and pour in enough rice for a small pancake. Cook for a few minutes until browned and crisp and arrange on a plate. Repeat with more pancakes. Serve with either maple syrup, liqueur, fresh fruit or ice cream.

OATMEAL FLAPJACKS

3/4 cup rolled oats (not instant)
1/2 cup flour
1 egg
1/2 tsp salt
1 tsp baking soda
Buttermilk to make a thick consistency
1 Tbsp oil

Mix all the above ingredients, except the oil, in a bowl. Heat the oil in a frypan and drop in spoonfuls of the mixture. Pat down and cook until slightly risen and lightly browned. Serve with whiskey, prune sauce.

✦ WHISKEY/PRUNE SAUCE

1 cup pitted prunes, chopped fine
3/4 cup water
1/2 tsp cinnamon

1/2 tsp ground ginger
2 tbsp honey or brown sugar or best of all, molasses.
2 Tbsps whiskey

Put everything in a saucepan deep enough to let it bubble up and simmer for five minutes.

If you want to make it a savoury sauce and spicier, add 1/2 tsp cayenne pepper. To make it stickier, for use on barbecued meat or chicken or fish, mix 1 Tbsp cornstarch with the whiskey and add it for the last 2 minutes of cooking.

YOU CAN DO IT WITH RYE BUT YOU WON'T BE ABLE TO GET YOUR KILT CLEANED !

PLATE SOUFFLÉ

4 egg whites - stiffly beaten
4 egg yolks - lightly beaten
2 Tbsps canned tomatoes
1 tsp tarragon or basil
1/2 tsp salt
Freshly ground pepper

Whisk the egg yolks and tomatoes together, add the tarragon, salt and pepper and gently fold in the egg whites using a metal spoon. Oil or butter an ovenproof plate and pour the souffle mixture onto it. Place in 450 F/220 C oven for 6-8 minutes until risen high in the middle. Serve immediately

SCRAMBLED EGGS

3 eggs
1/2 tsp salt
Freshly ground pepper
1 Tbsp finely chopped green onion
1 Tbsp butter
1/2 eggshell of cream

Beat the eggs lightly with the salt, pepper and green onion. Melt the butter in a pan over a low to medium heat and pour in the eggs. Stir gently, add the cream and remove from the heat when still slightly runny, just before they are set. Serve immediately.

SCRAMBLED EGGS WITH COUSCOUS

1 cup couscous
1 1/2 cups water
1 tsp butter
4 eggs
1/2 tsp salt
Freshly ground pepper
1 Tbsp butter
1 Tbsp finely chopped onion
1/2 red pepper - diced
1 Tbsp chopped parsley
1/2 tsp cinnamon
1/2 tsp paprika
1/2 eggshell milk

Put the couscous into a saucepan (with the heat off) and pour over the 1 1/2 cups of boiling water. Put the lid on and let it steam for 5 minutes. Add 1 tsp butter, fluff up with a fork and keep warm. Meanwhile melt 1 Tbsp butter in a pan and stir in the onion and red pepper. Break the eggs into a bowl, add salt and pepper and beat lightly. Pour into the pan and stir gently. Add 1/2 eggshell of milk, the cinnamon and paprika and remove from the heat just before the eggs set. Serve the couscous heaped on a platter, make a hole in the middle and pour in the scrambled eggs. Scatter with chopped parsley.

CORN, EGGS AND TOMATOES

1 dozen eggs
1 tsp salt
1/2 tsp cayenne pepper
1 onion - chopped
1 green pepper - chopped
1 red pepper - chopped
1/2 cup black olives
1 Tbsp chopped garlic
2 Tbsps chopped parsley
1 can corn or 1 packet frozen corn
Grated cheese
Tomato halves

Beat the eggs in a large bowl and stir in all the remaining ingredients - except the tomatoes and cheese. Pour into a greased baking dish, lay the tomato halves on top and bake in a 350 F/180 C oven for about 20-30 minutes. Halfway through, sprinkle the top with grated cheese and put back in the oven. Serve with hot biscuits

HOT BISCUITS

2 cups flour
1 tsp salt
1 Tbsp baking powder
1 tsp baking soda
1 cup sour cream or buttermilk
1/2 tsp paprika
2 handfuls grated cheese

Mix the flour, salt, baking powder and baking soda together in a large bowl. Stir in the sour cream, paprika and cheese and mix well. Pat out the dough onto a floured board and roll out to 1/2" thickness. Cut out rounds with a cookie cutter or wine glass, place on a greased baking sheet and bake in a 350 F/180 C oven for 10-15 minutes.

THE URBAN PEASANT

BAKED POTATOES AND EGGS

2 potatoes
4 eggs

Prick 2 potatoes and microwave at half power for 5 minutes. Remove, cut in half and spoon out some of the insides leaving a shell large enough to fit an egg. Break an egg into each half and return to the microwave for 3 minutes. Serve immediately.

HOME-MADE BREAKFAST SAUSAGE

1/2 lb/250g ground pork
1 apple, grated
1 onion, grated
1 tsp flour
1/2 tsp sage
1 tsp pepper
1/2 tsp salt
1 Tbsp oil

Mix together in a bowl and form into small cakes. Fry in hot oil until browned and serve for breakfast with eggs.

EGG FOO YONG

1 onion - finely chopped
1 Tbsp oil
1 stick celery - finely chopped
1 carrot - finely chopped
1 clove garlic - finely chopped
1/2 lb/250g fresh shrimp or canned
6 eggs
1/2 tsp salt
Freshly ground pepper
2 handfuls beansprouts

Heat the oil in a frypan and sauté the onion, celery, carrot and garlic. When cooked, add the shrimp and heat through, remove from the heat and make the omelette. Break the eggs into a bowl, add salt & pepper and the beansprouts. Heat a little oil in a frypan and pour in the egg and sprouts mixture. Cook for 2 minutes until set. Slide out half-way onto a plate, spoon the shrimp mixture onto it and fold over the other half. Garnish with cilantro.

TOAD IN THE HOLE

1/2 lb/250g sausages
2 eggs
1 cup flour
1/2 tsp salt
1 cup milk

Fry the sausages in a hot frypan until brown. Beat the eggs in a bowl until frothy. Stir in the flour and salt and gradually add the milk to make a smooth batter. Pour the batter into the hot pan and put in a 400 F/220 C oven for 20-30 minutes. A slower oven just won't work.

BANGERS & MASH

Mash some boiled potatoes with 1 Tbsp butter, freshly ground pepper and 1 Tbsp chopped parsley. Prick some sausages with a fork and fry either in 2 Tbsps water in a hot frypan or in a dry pan over medium heat. When browned, serve either as a "hedgehog", with the sausages poked into a mound of mashed potatoes or serve with mashed potatoes and caramelized onion rings on the side.

ONION RINGS

2 Tbsps oil
2 onions - thinly sliced
1 tsp vinegar
1 tsp caraway seeds

Heat the oil in a frypan and sauté the onion rings until browned and caramelized. Sprinkle with the vinegar and caraway seeds, stir well and serve with bangers and mash.

TOFU & OYSTER SAUCE

1 packet medium tofu
2 Tbsps oil
1/2 onion - coarsely chopped
2 cloves garlic - chopped
1/2 tsp cayenne
Freshly ground pepper
4-5 slices ginger
1 Tbsp sesame oil
1 tsp oyster sauce
2 green onions - chopped

Heat the oil in a frypan and sauté the onions and garlic over high heat. Cut the tofu into cubes and add to the pan with the ginger. Sprinkle with cayenne pepper and freshly ground pepper and gently move the tofu around without breaking it up. When the tofu is coloured pour in the sesame oil, oyster sauce and chopped green onion. Cook for a further 1-2 minutes and serve.

RATATOUILLE

4 Tbsps olive oil
2 onions - coarsely chopped
3 large tomatoes - sliced thickly
2 zucchini - cut into chunks
1 eggplant - cut into chunks
1 tsp basil
1 tsp oregano
6 cloves garlic - whole
1 Tbsp chopped parsley
1 Tbsp tomato paste

Freshly ground pepper
1 Tbsp vinegar

Heat the oil in a large sauté pan over high heat. Stir in the onions, tomatoes, zucchini and eggplant. Make sure everything is coated with oil and add the garlic cloves, herbs and tomato paste. Stir well, put the lid on, turn down the heat and simmer for 30 minutes. Stir in the vinegar 5 minutes before finishing. Serve with chopped parsley.

SPICY CHINESE EGGPLANT

2-3 oriental eggplants - cut into chunks
3 Tbsps oil
1/2 onion - chopped
1/2 red pepper - chopped
1/2 green pepper - chopped
5-6 whole, hot peppers
1/2 tsp salt
1/2 tsp sugar
1 Tbsp soy sauce
1 Tbsp black bean sauce
1 tsp tomato paste
1 tsp sesame oil

Heat the oil in a frypan over high heat and sauté the onions until transparent. Stir in the eggplant until coloured and add the rest of the ingredients leaving the sesame oil to the end. Stir well, keeping the heat high, for 5-6 minutes. Stir in the sesame oil and serve.

EGGPLANT GRILLED WITH MOZZARELLA

Crisp-fry thick slices of eggplant. Lay mozzarella slices over the eggplant with some chopped garlic and freshly ground pepper. Sandwich 2 pieces of eggplant together and broil until the mozzarella just melts, about 2-3 minutes. Serve.

PEPPER STEW

1 red pepper
1 green pepper
1 yellow pepper
1 red onion - coarsely chopped
3 cloves of garlic - roughly chopped
1 tin anchovies
1 tsp oregano
Freshly ground pepper
3 Tbsps olive oil
1 Tbsp vinegar

Heat up a frypan and pour in the olive oil. Tear up the 3 peppers into pieces or chop coarsely and add to the pan with the chopped onion. Stir in the garlic, the anchovies, freshly ground pepper and oregano until the anchovies melt and simmer gently with the lid on for about 15 minutes. Stir in the vinegar, cook 30 seconds and serve, hot, cold or lukewarm.

BLACK-EYED PEA CURRY

2 Tbsps oil
1 onion - coarsely chopped
5-6 cardamom pods
1 Tbsp curry powder
2 Tbsps chopped tomatoes
1 Tbsp chopped red pepper
1 Tbsp chopped carrot
1 can black-eyed peas & 1 can water
1/2 tsp salt
2 hot, red peppers

Heat the oil in a large sauté pan and brown the onions and cardamom pods. Stir in the curry powder, tomatoes, red pepper and carrot. Wash and rinse the peas well and pour into the pan along with 1 can of water. Bring back to the boil and simmer for 10 minutes with the lid on. Five minutes before serving, add the salt and hot, red peppers. Serve with rice and chopped cilantro.

FRIED RICE JAVANESE STYLE

2 Tbsps oil
2 sticks celery - chopped
1/2 red pepper - chopped
1/2 green pepper - chopped
1 onion - coarsely chopped
3 slices ginger
1 carrot - chopped
1 hot, red pepper
1 small bunch green onions
1 clove garlic - chopped
1 cup cold, cooked rice
1 tsp turmeric

Heat up the oil in a large frypan and fry the onions, celery, carrot, ginger slices, green and red pepper. Add the cold rice and turmeric and stir well. Cut the green onions into 1" lengths, reserving the green ends for decoration, and add with the chopped, hot red pepper. Put in some freshly ground pepper and stir well for a few minutes. Serve garnished with chopped green onion and strips of omelette.

✒ OMELETTE

1 egg
1/2 eggshell water
1 Tbsp oil or butter.

Heat up the oil in a small frypan. Beat the egg and water and pour into the pan. Shake around to make the omelette nice and thin. Slide out when cooked onto a board. Drizzle a little oil over and gently roll up. Cut across into slices and use to garnish the Fried Rice Javanese Style.

SALAD NICOISE

2 cups cold, cooked rice
1/2 romaine lettuce - leaves torn up
1/2 lb/250g cherry tomatoes
1 avocado - chopped
1/2 red pepper - diced
2 sticks celery - chopped
2 Tbsps black olives
1 can anchovies
2-3 hard-boiled eggs

Toss all the above ingredients together. Take a small jar and pour in 2" of olive oil, 1/2" vinegar, pinch cayenne and 1/2 tsp thyme, put the lid on, shake well and pour over the salad.

ZUCCHINI LATKES WITH TOMATO PASTE SAUCE AND THIN YOGHURT

2 zucchinis, grated
1 Tbsp flour
1 tsp pepper
1 tsp tarragon
1 egg
2 Tbsps olive oil
3 Tbsps yoghurt
1 tsp tomato paste
Juice of 1/2 lemon

Stir together the grated zucchini, flour, tarragon and pepper in a bowl and mix in the egg. Heat the oil in a frypan over medium heat and put spoonfuls of the mixture into the pan. Pat down and fry until brown on each side. Mix the yoghurt, tomato paste and lemon juice together to form a sauce. Pour onto a plate and arrange the cooked latkes on top.

SUCCOTASH

2 Tbsps vegetable oil or butter.
2 onions, cut into 1/8ths
1 carrot, cut into finger thick slices.
2 bell peppers, chopped coarsely
6 ripe tomatoes, whole or chopped
3 cloves of garlic
2 cobs of corn, cut crosswise into slices two fingers thick.
1 turnip, peeled & chopped
1 cup of pumpkin or squash chunks
1 broccoli head
3 tsps seasonings - 1 of dill, 1 of thyme, 1 of ground pepper
1 tsp salt
3 cups cider, stock or water
1 tsp salt

Heat the oil in a large saucepan over high heat. Add onions, stir well for 30 seconds, then the carrots, squash and turnip (heat still high) and stir them energetically, up from the bottom of the pan. When they are coated with hot oil, add all the seasonings. Stir it all well together until shiny, (the heat still high) then add the cider or stock. When boiling, add the corn, tomatoes and broccoli, cover and cook for 6 minutes. Look occasionally, and if it needs a little more liquid, add some, but remember that the real pleasure of this stew comes from the juices of the vegetables.

QUICK PASTA FAGIOLI

2 Tbsps olive oil
1 can white beans (or 1 cup dried white beans, soaked overnight and simmered an hour until done)
1 cup short pasta (like elbow macaroni) or any broken pasta
1 onion, grated
1 small carrot, grated
1/2 lb/250g ground turkey
1 handful parsley, chopped
Pepper and salt
1 bay leaf
1 tsp oregano
Water, bean water or stock

Heat the oil in a large saucepan and brown the meat. Grind in some black pepper and stir well. Add the grated onion and carrot, bay leaf, oregano, beans, pasta and 1 cup of bean water. Cover and cook for 15-20 minutes or until the pasta is done. Add more stock if necessary as it should be like soup. Add salt to taste. Aficionados eat it well dusted with grated parmesan.

TAGLIATELLE ALLE OLIVE

Pasta, enough for four people
3 Tbsps olive oil
3 cloves garlic, crushed
1 cup black olives
3 Tbsps parsley, chopped
1/2 tsp chilli flakes
1 tsp ground black pepper
Salt to taste
Juice 1/2 lemon
2 Tbsp grated parmesan

Cook the pasta and drain. While it's cooking, pit the olives and chop coarsely. Mix with the olive oil, garlic, chilli flakes, pepper, parmesan cheese and lemon juice. Add to the hot pasta, toss, sprinkle copiously with parsley, add salt if necessary, and serve immediately.

POTATO PIZZA

2 large potatoes, peeled & cooked
1 Tbsp butter
1/4 cup cheese (parmesan or grated cheddar)
1 egg
1/2 tsp salt
1 tsp pepper
Chopped parsley

Mash the potatoes and butter and mix in the cheese, egg, salt, pepper and parsley. Flour a pie plate or pizza pan, press in the potato mixture and smooth the top, leaving a slightly raised edge. Sprinkle with whatever pizza toppings you wish; some grated cheese, cheddar or fine cut mozzarella, sliced tomatoes, sliced mushrooms, green pepper, anchovies, olives or whatever you like. Bake for 20 minutes in a 450F/230C oven.

DAL

1 cup small orange lentils
2 cups water
1 onion, finely chopped
3 cloves garlic, finely chopped
6 slices ginger
2 Tbsps oil
1 cup water
1 cup yoghurt
1 tsp curry powder
1/2 tsp cayenne pepper or dried chillies
Juice of 1 lemon
1/2 cup grated coconut
1/2 tsp salt
1 tsp pepper
Chopped coriander

Cook the lentils in 2 cups of water for 15-20 minutes. In a frypan, heat the oil and fry the onion, garlic, ginger and pepper until the onion has browned. Stir in the curry powder, cayenne and coconut until well mixed. Add the cooked lentils, salt and lemon juice and stir in the yoghurt. Cook for a further 2-3 minutes, remove the pieces of ginger and serve garnished with chopped coriander and grated coconut.

VEGGIES

ASPARAGUS STEAMED IN A COFFEE POT

Break off the stringy ends of a bunch of asparagus. Pour about a cup of water into an electric coffee pot, put in the asparagus, replace the lid and plug in. Cook 5-7 minutes, depending on the size of the asparagus. Pour off the water and shake the asparagus out of the pot onto a plate.

ASPARAGUS & GINGER

Break off the stringy ends of a bunch of asparagus. Melt 1 tsp. butter in a frying pan and add 4 slices of fresh ginger. Put in the asparagus and sprinkle over a pinch of salt. Cover and cook 3-4 minutes, until just crunchy. Squeeze lemon juice over and serve with the pan sauce.

ASPARAGUS AND DILL

Break off the stringy ends of a bunch of asparagus, lay out flat on a board and cut them into thin long diagonals. Heat 1 Tbsp oil in a pan on a high heat and when hot put in the asparagus and toss. Sprinkle with salt. Cook for 2-3 minutes. Serve with a yoghurt and dill sauce. (Mix 3 Tbsps yoghurt with some chopped fresh dill and garnish with dill sprigs).

ASPARAGUS ORIENTAL

1 bunch asparagus - stringy ends removed
1 tsp butter
2-3 slices ginger- julienned
1/2 tsp salt
Splash of sherry

Cut the asparagus lengthwise, turning the asparagus all the time to produce a 'rolling cut'. Melt the butter in a frypan and stir in the ginger. Immediately add the asparagus, stir well and sprinkle with salt. Add a splash of sherry, put the lid on and cook for 30 seconds. Remove from the heat and serve.

ASPARAGUS PARMIGIANA

1 bunch asparagus
2 Tbsps olive oil
1/2 tsp salt
1 Tbsp butter
1/2 cup breadcrumbs
1/2 tsp pepper
Parmesan cheese

Heat the oil in a frypan. Break off the stringy ends of the asparagus and lay in the hot oil. Sprinkle with salt, cover and cook for 2 minutes or until tender. Remove to a plate. Melt the butter in the frypan and brown the breadcrumbs. Sprinkle with pepper, stir and tip out onto the asparagus. Garnish with grated parmesan cheese.

ASPARAGUS STEAMED IN A FRYPAN

Break the stringy ends off a bunch of asparagus. Pour 1/2" water into a frypan and bring to the boil. Lay the asparagus in, sprinkle with salt, put the lid on and steam for 3 minutes. Drain and arrange on a plate drizzled with hollandaise sauce and garnished with chopped hard-boiled egg.

➤ QUICK HOLLANDAISE SAUCE

3 egg yolks
1/2 cup hot, melted butter
1/2 lemon
1/2 tsp dry mustard
Salt

Blend the egg yolks on high speed until pale yellow and frothy. Keep the blender going and quickly pour in the hot, melted butter, the lemon juice, salt and mustard and when thickened, pour over the asparagus.

ASPARAGUS JAPANESE STYLE

2 Tbsps olive oil
2-3 slices fresh ginger - chopped
1/2 tsp salt
1 bunch asparagus - stringy ends removed, halved lengthwise.
1 Tbsp rice vinegar
1 tsp sugar
Pinch cayenne pepper
Sesame seeds

Heat the oil in a frypan and stir in the chopped ginger. Add the asparagus, sprinkle with salt, toss lightly and put the lid on. Cook for 2 minutes. Pour in the rice vinegar and sugar, stir quickly and serve sprinkled with cayenne pepper and black and white sesame seeds.

ASPARAGUS FRENCH STYLE

1 tsp butter
1 bunch asparagus - stringy ends removed
1/2 tsp salt
2 Tbsps cream
1 tsp tarragon

Melt the butter in a frypan and lay in the asparagus. Toss it well in the butter, put the lid on and cook for 3 minutes. Pour off any extra butter and add the cream and tarragon. Stir and serve.

ASPARAGUS CHINESE STYLE

1 Tbsp oil
2 Tbsps ground beef
1/2 chopped onion
2 Tbsps chopped fresh ginger
2-3 cloves chopped garlic
1 tsp dried chillies
6 asparagus spears - cut diagonally into thin bite size pieces
2 Tbsps black bean sauce

1/2 tsp salt
2 Tbsps water or sherry

Heat the oil in a frypan and brown the meat. Stir in the onion, ginger, garlic and chillies and cook for 5 minutes. Add the asparagus, black bean sauce, salt and water and stir well keeping the heat high for another 2 minutes. Serve.

CURRIED ASPARAGUS EGGS WITH DILL

4 eggs
1/2 tsp curry powder
1/2 tsp dill
1 Tbsp butter
1 bunch asparagus, stringy ends removed
2 Tbsps chopped, green onions
Salt & pepper
Juice of 1/2 lemon

Melt the butter in a frypan and stir in the curry powder. Cut the asparagus diagonally and add them to the pan. Squeeze in some lemon juice and when the asparagus is three quarters cooked, remove to a warm plate. Lightly beat the eggs and some black pepper and add the chopped onions. Pour the eggs into the frypan, stirring gently. When the eggs start to set, tip in the asparagus, stir and serve immediately.

ASPARAGUS & CASHEW STIRFRY (Or Almonds)

1 bunch asparagus, stringy ends removed and cut into thirds
2 Tbsps oil
1/2 cup almonds or cashews
2 Tbsps white wine
1/2 yellow pepper, diced
1 tsp sesame oil

Heat the oil in a frypan over high heat and sauté the almonds or cashews until browned. Add the asparagus, sprinkle with a little salt to keep green, and pour in the wine. Stir and add the diced yellow pepper. Tip onto a plate and drizzle over the sesame oil.

ASPARAGUS & CARROTS

1 Tbsp oil
1 Tbsp grated, fresh ginger
1 bunch asparagus - stringy ends removed
1/2 tsp salt
1 Tbsp frozen orange juice or juice of an orange
1 carrot - grated
1 Tbsp sesame oil
Freshly ground pepper

Heat the oil in a frypan over a high heat and stir in the grated ginger. Add the asparagus and move it gently around to coat each spear with the ginger and oil. Sprinkle in the salt and add the orange juice. Put the lid on, turn the heat down and simmer for 3 minutes. Stir in the grated carrot for one minute and finally stir in the sesame oil and pepper. Serve.

GREEN BEANS OR ASPARAGUS MAITRE D'HOTEL

Mash together, some softened butter, finely chopped parsley and 1 Tbsp lemon or orange juice. Wrap in waxed paper and chill. Slice and serve with asparagus or green beans, which have been put into boiling, salted water and cooked for 4 minutes. You could also mix a little curry powder into the butter, or hot, red pepper for spice.

HOT GREEN BEAN & MUSHROOM SALAD

1 lb/500g green beans
1/2 lb/250g mushrooms, sliced
French dressing

Steam the beans and drain. Make a French dressing using twice the amount of oil to vinegar and a pinch of salt and pepper. Toss the beans with the mushrooms and dressing while still warm and garnish with chopped parsley.

CAULIFLOWER SALAD

2 heads cauliflower, broken into florets
1 cup chopped parsley
2 cloves chopped garlic
2 Tbsps capers
1 can anchovies
1/2 cup lemon juice
3/4 cup olive oil
1 tsp orange zest

Mix the cauliflower, parsley and capers together in a salad bowl. Blend the anchovies, garlic, lemon juice, orange zest and olive oil and toss with the cauliflower. Decorate with some more orange zest.

SPINACH, ORANGE & WALNUT SALAD

1 large bunch fresh spinach
2 oranges
1 cup walnut halves
2 Tbsp good olive oil
1 tsp fresh ground pepper
1/2 tsp salt
1 tsp dill
1 cup crumbled feta cheese or 1 cup cottage cheese mixed with a sprinkle of vinegar

Put walnuts in a frypan over medium heat, and cook 3 minutes, shaking occasionally. Meanwhile wash, dry and coarsely chop spinach. Peel the oranges and cut each section into 3 pieces. Take walnuts off heat. Put oranges and spinach into bowl, toss with olive oil and pepper, sprinkle with salt and a little green dill. If using feta, toss it into the salad, if cottage cheese then arrange round the rim of the bowl. Eat immediately — spinach leaves absorb orange juice and oil and can get soggy.

WALDORF SALAD

1/2 cup shelled walnuts - roasted
2 apples - cored & quartered
1/2 head celery - cut crosswise

Small bunch green grapes
2 Tbsp yoghurt
1/2 tsp salt
Freshly ground pepper

Put the apple quarters into a bowl of "acidulated water" (water and lemon juice) to stop them browning. Put the celery pieces into a large salad bowl and add the roasted walnuts. Chop the apple quarters into chunks and place in the bowl along with the green grapes. Put in the yoghurt and toss with a little grated cheese and some parsley.

SPINACH AU GRATIN

1 packet of frozen spinach
1 tsp butter
1 tsp red pepper
1 clove garlic - chopped
1/2 cup toasted walnuts
1/2 cup of grated cheese & breadcrumbs

Cut the frozen spinach into pieces. Butter a small gratin dish and put in the spinach. Dot with the butter. Add the chopped garlic, roasted walnuts and the hot pepper and finish with the mixture of cheese & breadcrumbs (or you could use just breadcrumbs & butter). Place in a toaster oven on high or broil until it is nicely browned. Sprinkle with dill and serve.

TOMATO & ONION SALAD

1 tomato - sliced
1 onion - sliced
1/2 tsp salt
Freshly ground pepper
2 Tbsps olive oil
1 tsp dill, thyme or oregano

Arrange the tomato slices on a plate. Add the onion rings and sprinkle with salt. Pour over the olive oil and grind some pepper over the top. Add dill, thyme or oregano and allow to stand for a short while.

COLE SLAW

1 onion - thinly sliced
1/2 cup sultanas
1/2 cup raisins
1/2 toasted walnuts
1/2 green cabbage - thinly sliced with a serrated edge knife

Dressing:

1/4 onion - finely chopped
3-4 Tbsps yoghurt
1 tsp freshly ground pepper
1 tsp dill
2 Tbsps finely chopped cucumber

Blanch the onion rings in boiling water for a few seconds. Remove and blanch the sultanas and raisins for a few minutes. In a large bowl mix the sliced cabbage, onion rings, sultanas and raisins. Chop the roasted walnuts and add these. Mix together all the ingredients for the dressing, toss this into the coleslaw and put in the fridge for about an hour before serving.

CAULIFLOWER CHEESE

1 cauliflower
2 Tbsps butter
1 1/2 Tbsps flour
1 cup milk
1/2 tsp salt
1/4 tsp cayenne
1/4 tsp grated nutmeg
1/4 cup grated cheese
1/4 cup breadcrumbs
1 slice ginger, julienned (optional)

Break the cauliflower into florets and steam for 1-2 minutes. Melt the butter in a saucepan and stir in the flour to make a roux. Slowly add the milk, stirring all the time until you have a creamy white sauce. Stir in the nutmeg, cayenne, salt, pepper and grated cheese. Put the cauliflower into a small dish and top with the cheese sauce. Sprinkle with breadcrumbs (or melt 1 Tbsp butter in a frypan, sauté the breadcrumbs and ginger and sprinkle these) and broil until brown and bubbling.

WILTED MUSHROOM & WALNUT SALAD

2 Tbsps olive oil
1/2 cup walnuts
2 cups chopped, old mushrooms
1 onion - thinly sliced
2 cloves garlic - finely chopped
1 Tbsp finely chopped parsley
1 Tbsp chopped green onion
Juice of 1/2 lemon
1/2 tsp cayenne pepper

Heat the oil in a frypan and add the walnuts. When they begin to 'pop' add the onion rings and stir. Add the chopped mushrooms, garlic, green onions, chopped parsley, cayenne pepper and lemon juice. Stir well and serve.

SUNOMONO

1/2 cucumber
1/2 tsp salt
1/2 tsp sugar
2-3 small prawns or 1 small can shrimps
1 tsp rice vinegar

Drag a fork down the outside of the cucumber all the way round and cut in thin slices (the edges will be serrated). Sprinkle with the salt and sugar and leave for a few minutes. Squeeze out the juice and arrange in a small bowl with the prawns or shrimps and sprinkle with the rice vinegar.

ZUCCHINI IN CARPIONE

1 medium zucchini, cut into long slices
2 slices fresh ginger, julienned
1 Tbsp olive oil
2 cloves garlic, chopped
1 tsp dried mint or chopped fresh mint
1/2 cup vinegar
Salt & pepper

Fry the zucchini slices and ginger in the hot oil until softened. Stir in the garlic and mint and add salt and pepper. Boil the vinegar in a saucepan and pour over the zucchini. Serve immediately or it will keep for a week in the fridge in a jar.

TOMATO AND SPINACH

1 can tomatoes
2 Tbsps butter
1/2 onion, chopped fine
1/2 tsp sugar
1 tsp dried oregano
1/4 cup whipping cream
1/2 pkg frozen chopped spinach
1/2 tsp dried basil
1/4 cup grated cheese

Sauté the onion in butter for 2 minutes. Stir in the rest of the ingredients except the cream and cheese and simmer until the spinach has melted. Blend in a food processor or blender and garnish with cream and cheese.

SPINACH & SESAME SEEDS

1 bunch fresh spinach - lightly steamed
Sesame seeds - roasted in a dry pan
Soy sauce

Tip out the sesame seeds onto a board. Form the spinach into long bundles about 1" across and roll them in the sesame seeds. Slice the rolls across into 1" pieces and arrange on a small plate. Sprinkle with soy sauce.

AVOCADO

Peel 1/2 avocado and slice, cutting not quite through to the end. Put on a plate and fan out gently, sprinkle with lemon juice, place a strawberry at the point and you have your own work of art.

RAW VEGETABLES WITH YOGHURT DIPS

YELLOW DIP

2 Tbsps peanut butter
Juice of an orange
2-3 Tbsps yoghurt

Put all the ingredients into a food processor and blend until smooth and creamy.

GREEN DIP

1 packet frozen spinach
2-3 Tbsps yoghurt

Cut up the frozen spinach and blend with the yoghurt in a food processor until smooth.

RED DIP

1 Tbsp tomato ketchup
1 Tbsp tomato paste
2-3 Tbsps yoghurt

Blend all the ingredients in a food processor until smooth. Serve all the above dips with a selection of raw vegetables.

BRUSSEL SPROUTS

Peel off the outside leaves of brussel sprouts and make a crosswise cut in the stalk end of each. Melt 1 tsp butter in a pan and add:

1 Tbsp almonds or walnuts
1/2 tsp salt
2 Tbsps water
       OR
1 Tbsp grainy mustard
1/2 tsp salt
2 Tbsps water
       OR
1 Tbsp peanut butter
1/2 tsp salt
1 Tbsps water

Put the lid on and cook for 6 - 8 minutes, shaking occasionally .

PAPAYA, PASTA & BASIL SALAD (With Papaya Seed Dressing)

1 papaya, cubed
1 bunch fresh basil, chopped
Cold, cooked pasta, lightly oiled

Mix all the above ingredients together and toss with the papaya seed dressing.

⤳ PAPAYA SEED DRESSING

1/2 cup vegetable oil
1/4 cup vinegar
1 Tbsp sugar
1/4 tsp salt
1/2 tsp dry mustard
1 Tbsp chopped onion
Seeds of 1 papaya
1 slice bread, optional

Mix all the ingredients in a blender and toss with the salad. The dressing will keep well in the fridge. Also add to cold, cooked rice for an unusual salad.

MANGETOUT SALAD

Mangetout (or sugar peas)
1 Tbsp oil
Juice of 1/2 lemon
Pinch of salt
Almonds

Blanch some mangetout for 2 minutes, strain and rinse with cold water. Mix together the oil, lemon juice and salt and pour over the mangetout. Sauté some almonds in a little butter and sprinkle over the top of the salad.

RED PEPPER & TOMATO APPETIZER

2 red peppers - halved
Cherry tomatoes - halved
1/2 tsp salt
Freshly ground pepper
1 tsp oregano, thyme or basil
1 Tbsp olive oil
Honey

Remove the seeds from the peppers and place in a greased baking dish. Fill each half with some cherry tomatoes and sprinkle over the salt, pepper, oregano and olive oil. Pour 1/2 tsp of liquid honey over each half and bake in a 350 F/180 C oven for 15-20 minutes.

CAULIFLOWER

1 cauliflower
2 Tbsps oil

1/2 tsp salt

nutmeg

Put in 1/8" water and 2 Tbsps oil into a frypan and heat. Break the cauliflower into florets and add to the pan, turn them over to coat thoroughly with oil. Sprinkle with salt and when the water starts to spit, put the lid on and simmer for 5 minutes. Serve sprinkled with nutmeg.

ZUCCHINI (Sixty Seconds)

1 zucchini - grated

1 tsp butter

2 cloves garlic - finely chopped

Juice of 1/2 lemon

Salt & pepper

Melt the butter in a small pan and add the garlic, zucchini, salt and pepper. Stir well over a high heat for a minute (no more than two), squeeze the lemon juice in and serve.

ORANGE & ONION SALAD

1 orange - thinly sliced

1 onion - thinly sliced

Freshly ground pepper

1/2 tsp salt

Olive oil

Arrange the orange and onion rings on a plate. Sprinkle with the salt and pepper and drizzle over some olive oil. Allow to sit and marinate for 10 minutes.

CHICORY & ORANGE SALAD

2 Tbsps roasted walnuts

2-3 heads of chicory

1 orange

Freshly ground pepper

Salt

Olive oil

Halve the chicory heads and remove the core. Slice the orange thinly. Arrange the chicory leaves and orange slices on a plate, scatter the walnuts over the top, sprinkle with salt and pepper and drizzle over some olive oil. Allow to sit for a few minutes and serve.

GREEN BEANS & YOGHURT

2 cups chopped green beans cut crosswise into bite size pieces

1 Tbsp yoghurt

1 Tbsp sesame oil

1/2 tsp salt

Pour 1/2" water into a frypan and when boiling put in the beans. Sprinkle with salt, stir and simmer with the lid on for 4 minutes. Strain the beans and toss with the yoghurt and sesame oil. Serve hot or cold.

INSALATA DI PEPERONIE CAPPERI

2 yellow peppers
2 Tbsps olive oil

Cut the peppers into long strips, heat the oil in a frypan and sauté over a high heat until limp. Tip onto a plate and serve with chilled tomato sauce:

2 tomatoes
2 cloves garlic
1 bunch fresh basil
1 bunch fresh mint
1/2 tsp salt
Freshly ground pepper
3-4 Tbsps olive oil

Put all the ingredients into a blender or food processor and mix. Chill well and serve over the hot, yellow peppers.

FRENCH WILTED CABBAGE SALAD

1 medium cabbage, cut into wedges & cored
8 slices bacon
1-2 Tbsps olive oil
Salt & pepper
2 Tbsps sherry (or vinegar)

Thinly shred the cabbage. Place in a saucepan of boiling water and steep for 5 minutes or until limp. Cut the bacon into strips and fry with the olive oil until crisp. Pour in the sherry and let bubble. Drain the cabbage and put in a dry bowl. Season with salt and lots of freshly ground black pepper. Pour over the bacon and drippings. Toss well and serve.

GHOBI AUR MATAR (Cauliflower & Peas)

1 cauliflower, broken into florets
1 cup peas
2 Tbsps oil
1 tsp black mustard seeds
1/2 tsp cumin seeds
1/2 tsp turmeric
1/2 tsp cayenne pepper
1/2 cup water
Juice of 1/2 lemon
Salt
Chopped coriander or mint leaves

Heat the oil in a frypan and add the mustard seeds and cumin seeds. When the mustard seeds have finished popping, add the cauliflower florets, cayenne, turmeric and water. Sauté for 5 minutes. Stir in the peas and salt, cover and cook for 2-3 minutes. Remove from heat, squeeze in the lemon juice and serve garnished with coriander or mint leaves.

SAUTÉED ARTICHOKE HEARTS

6 artichokes, outer leaves removed
3-4 Tbsps olive oil
10 whole cloves garlic, unpeeled
Juice of 1/2 lemon
Orange slices
Salt & pepper

Cut the artichokes horizontally across the bottom and top of the leaves and rub with lemon. Heat the oil in a frypan and lay in the artichoke hearts and garlic cloves. Squeeze over the lemon juice, sprinkle with salt and pepper, cover and cook for 10-15 minutes. Place each artichoke heart on a slice of orange and serve.

SPINACH & BANANA SALAD

2-3 Tbsps yoghurt
1 Tbsp sesame seeds
1/2 lemon
Freshly ground pepper
1 banana - cut into chunks
Fresh spinach leaves

Stir the yoghurt, sesame seeds and lemon juice together to make a dressing. Mix the banana chunks with the spinach leaves in a large salad bowl and toss with the dressing. Sprinkle with some more sesame seeds.

GREEN BEANS VINAIGRETTE

2 handfuls of fresh, green beans
Olive oil
Vinegar
Pinch salt
1/2 tsp grated nutmeg
1 tsp thyme
1/4 lb/125g gruyere cheese - cubed

Top and tail the beans and blanch in boiling water for 4 minutes. Half-fill an empty spice jar with olive oil and pour in some vinegar to give 3 times the amount of oil to vinegar. Add the salt, nutmeg and thyme, put the lid on and shake well. Drain the beans and toss with the dressing. Leave to marinate for 10 minutes and mix with the cheese.

SPINACH CRUMBLE

1 bunch fresh spinach
1 cup toasted walnuts - chopped
1 cup breadcrumbs
2 Tbsps olive oil
1 tsp basil
Freshly ground pepper

Wash the spinach and put in a large sauté pan with no extra water. Cook with the lid on for 4 minutes or until the leaves are limp. Drain well, mix with the chopped walnuts, press into a greased baking dish and sprinkle with a little olive oil and pepper. Toss 2 Tbsps olive oil, the breadcrumbs and basil together and sprinkle over the top. Bake in a 375 F/190 C oven for 5 minutes or until the top is golden brown.

CAULIFLOWER POLONAISE

1 cauliflower - broken into florets
2 Tbsps olive oil
1/2 tsp salt
1 tsp grated nutmeg
Freshly ground pepper

Pour 1/8" of water and 2 Tbsps olive oil into a frypan and bring to a boil. Add the cauliflower florets, toss and sprinkle with salt and pepper. Put the lid on and cook for 2-3 minutes. Drain and serve sprinkled with grated nutmeg.

LEEKS & GINGER

6 leeks
2 Tbsps oil
3 slices ginger - julienned
1 Tbsp water
1 tsp grated nutmeg

Cut the tops off the leeks, cut lengthwise and open out. Clean under a running tap. Heat the oil and water in a frypan and put in the ginger. When hot add the leeks and cook for 3-5 minutes. Sprinkle with grated nutmeg and serve hot or cold.

WILTED SPINACH

3-4 slices bacon - chopped
2 Tbsps chives - chopped
Freshly ground pepper
Fresh spinach leaves
1 Tbsp vinegar

Wash the spinach leaves, pat dry and place in a salad bowl. Fry the bacon in a frypan over high heat. Add the chives and pepper and stir. When the bacon is brown and crisp, strain the fat off, reserving 1 tsp, and replace the bacon in the frypan along with the 1 tsp of fat. Add the vinegar, stir once and pour onto the spinach leaves. Toss well and serve immediately.

FENNEL & ORANGE

2 fennel bulbs
1 orange - peeled & segmented
1/2 tsp salt
2 Tbsps olive oil
Freshly ground pepper

Quarter the fennel lengthwise, turn over and slice crosswise. Pile onto a plate and sprinkle with the salt, pepper and olive oil. Add the orange segments and toss well. Marinate for a few minutes and serve.

CURRIED CANTALOUPE

1 melon - flesh scooped out and cubed
1 cucumber - cubed

1 lemon
1 tsp curry powder
2 Tbsps oil
1/2 tsp salt

Put the melon and cucumber chunks in a bowl. Stir together in a frypan over medium heat the oil, lemon juice, curry powder and salt. When it is hot and everything melted, pour over the melon and cucumber and toss. Serve in the hollowed out melon.

PARSNIPS & SESAME SEEDS

3 parsnips - peeled and cut into lengths
1 Tbsp oil
1 Tbsp sesame seeds
1 Tbsp soy sauce
1 tsp butter
Chopped parsley

Heat the oil over a 350 F/180 C heat and fry the parsnips until golden coloured. Sprinkle in the sesame seeds and stir in the soy sauce and butter. Cook for 2 minutes and serve garnished with chopped parsley.

INDONESIAN SALAD GADO GADO

2 Tbsps oil
2 cloves garlic - chopped
1 tsp dried chillies
1 Tbsp soy sauce
1 Tbsp vinegar
3-4 slices ginger - chopped
1-2 Tbsps peanut butter
Blanched mixed vegetables

Heat the oil in a frypan and heat all the above ingredients until the peanut butter melts and makes a sauce. Keep warm. Quickly blanch a selection of fresh vegetables such as asparagus, green beans, cauliflower and broccoli florets, cabbage and bean sprouts. Strain well and arrange on a platter. Pour the hot sauce over the top of them, squeeze over some lemon juice and garnish with chopped hard boiled eggs and chopped parsley.

RED CABBAGE

1 red cabbage
2 Tbsps oil (or leftover duck fat)
1/2 onion - finely chopped
1-2 apples - chopped
2 Tbsps currants
1 Tbsp sugar
1/2 tsp salt
2 Tbsps vinegar

Heat the oil in a large sauté pan and add the cabbage. Stir in the remaining ingredients, turn down the heat and simmer, with the lid on, for 20-30 minutes.

PEAS & LETTUCE

Lettuce leaves - with spine removed for easier handling
1 small packet frozen peas
1 tsp butter
1 tsp mint
1 tsp sugar
1 tsp salt
2 Tbsp water
Salt & pepper

Line a small pan with half of the lettuce leaves. Tip in the frozen peas, butter, mint, salt and pepper and top with the remaining lettuce leaves. Put the lid on and cook over moderate heat for about 5 minutes.

CORN OFF THE COB

1 fresh corn on the cob
1 tsp butter
1 Tbsp red pepper - diced
Salt & pepper

Melt the butter in a small frypan. Cut the corn off the cob with a sharp knife and add to the pan. Stir in the diced red pepper and seasoning, put the lid on tight and cook for about 3 minutes.

PARSNIPS

1 parsnip
1 tsp butter
2-3 slices ginger - chopped
2 Tbsps water
Salt & pepper

Melt the butter in a small frypan. Stir in the chopped ginger. Cut the parsnip into lengths resembling french fries and add to the pan. Put in 2 Tbsps water and a pinch of salt & pepper. Stir and cook for about 3 minutes.

CARROTS & DILL

1 tsp butter
1-2 Tbsps brown sugar
1 tsp dill
1 lb small carrots
1/2 cup beer

Melt the butter in a saucepan and add the brown sugar. When it's melted and sticky add the dill. As soon as it bubbles, add the carrots and stir to coat them with the sugary sauce. Pour in the beer, turn down the heat and simmer with the lid on for about 10 minutes.

CANDIED CARROT STICKS

3-4 peeled carrots
1 tsp butter

1 Tbsp brown sugar
Juice of 1/2 orange
Red cabbage leaves
2 Tbsps cottage cheese
Freshly ground pepper
Sesame seeds

Halve the carrots and slice lengthwise into sticks. Melt the butter in a frypan and immediately add the carrot sticks. Stir well to make sure they are all coated with butter and add the brown sugar and orange juice. Allow to caramelize over medium heat. Place a cabbage leaf in a small bowl, spoon the cottage cheese into the bottom and grind some pepper over. Arrange the candied carrot sticks on top and sprinkle with sesame seeds.

BANANA & NUT SALAD

2 bananas
Romaine lettuce
Peanut butter
2 Tbsps roasted nuts - e.g. peanuts, cashews, almonds or walnuts
1 orange - peeled & sliced

Remove the core from the lettuce and either lay whole leaves on a plate or chop up. Peel and cut the bananas in half lengthwise, spread with peanut butter and lay them on top of the lettuce. Sprinkle over the toasted nuts and garnish with twists of orange.

CAESAR SALAD

1 romaine lettuce, shredded
1 ripe avocado
1 tsp dijon mustard
Juice of 1/2 lemon
1 tsp pepper
2 Tbsps olive oil
3-4 anchovies

Blend the avocado, mustard, lemon juice, pepper, oil and anchovies until smooth, adding wine or apple juice if necessary. Just before serving, toss with the shredded romaine lettuce and garnish with croutons which have been fried with garlic and oil.

MANGETOUT & TOMATOES

2 cups mangetout or sugar peas
2 cups cherry tomatoes
1 cup feta cheese
1 cup blueberries
2 Tbsps olive oil
Juice of 1/2 lemon or orange
1 tsp oregano or thyme

Heat the oil in a frypan and quick fry the mangetout. Stir in the cherry tomatoes and oregano or thyme. Sprinkle with the lemon or orange juice, stir quickly and pour out onto a plate. Scatter crumbled feta cheese over and garnish with the blueberries.

SCRAMBLED TOFU ON EGGPLANT SLICES

1 packet firm tofu
1 Tbsp chopped tarragon
2 green onion, chopped
2 large eggplants
2 Tbsp olive oil
Salt & pepper
1 Tbsp oil

Blend tofu, herbs and olive oil in a food processor. Slice the eggplants lengthwise, brush with a little olive oil and season. Heat the frypan and fry the slices until browned well on both sides without being limp. Serve the eggplant slices topped with the tofu mixture and garnish with red pepper and parsley.

GREAT TOMATO SALAD

1 red onion, thinly sliced
2 red tomatoes, sliced
2 yellow tomatoes, sliced
Fresh basil, or dried
Fresh parsley, or dried
Fresh oregano, or dried
Pinch of salt
Pinch of sugar
2 Tbsps olive oil
Freshly ground black pepper.

Arrange on a large platter, drizzle over the olive oil and grind over lots of freshly ground black pepper.

FRIED GREEN TOMATOES

Green tomatoes
1/2 cup flour
1 tsp oregano
1/2 tsp salt
1/2 tsp pepper
3-4 rashers bacon

Fry the bacon until crispy and remove from the pan. Mix the flour, oregano, salt and pepper together. Slice the tomatoes fairly thick and dip them in the flour. Fry in the bacon fat and serve for breakfast with bacon and eggs.

ZUCCHINI WITH WALNUTS

2 zucchini, sliced finger thick
1 med onion, sliced thin
2 Tbsps oil
1/2 cup chopped walnuts
1 Tbsp frozen orange juice
Salt & pepper
1/2 tsp tarragon

Heat the oil in a frypan and quick fry the onion slices over a high heat. Add the walnuts, toss for 1-2 minutes and add the zucchini slices. When lightly browned, stir in the orange juice, salt, pepper and tarragon, cook for 1 minute and serve.

FRESH CORN ON THE COB

Soak the unpeeled corn in cold water for 10-20 minutes. Either cook them (unpeeled) in a 500F/250C oven for 10-15 minutes, or microwave (unpeeled) at full power for 4 minutes. When microwaving, place the corn on a damp tea towel.

THAI CUCUMBER SALAD

1 cucumber, thinly sliced or grated
4 Tbsp sugar
2 Tbsp vinegar
1 small onion, sliced very thin
1 tsp finely chopped hot red pepper or 1/2 tsp dry red pepper
Fresh coriander
1 bunch radishes sliced thin.
Sesame seeds

Sprinkle cucumber with half of the sugar and let stand for 3-4 minutes. Wring out with hands, combine with the hot, red pepper, vinegar and remaining sugar and salt to taste. Garnish with chopped coriander and radishes and refrigerate until ready. Garnish with black or white sesame seeds (put them on last as you don't want them to get soggy).

GREEN BEANS & COCONUT

Blanch some fresh green beans for 3-4 minutes. Drain and toss with salt and pepper. Top with a diced tomato and grated coconut and drizzle with 2 Tbsps olive oil mixed with 1 tsp sherry.

BROCCOLI & CORN STIR-FRY

1 head of broccoli
1 fresh corn on the cob, or 1 can corn kernels or 1 packet frozen corn
4-5 whole, hot, red chillies or 1 tsp dried chilli flakes
1 small onion, chopped
3 slices fresh ginger, julienned
3 cloves garlic, chopped
1 Tbsp oil
1/3 cup liquid
1/2 tsp salt

Heat the oil in a frypan and sauté the ginger, garlic and chillies. Stir in the broccoli, sprinkle with salt and cook for 1-2 minutes. Add the corn and liquid and cook another 1-2 minutes. Serve hot.

CARROT & ORANGE SALAD

2 oranges
2 carrots, peeled & grated
1 tsp ground cinnamon

Juice of 1/2 orange

1 tsp honey

1 Tbsp chopped mint leaves

Salt & pepper

Zest of 1/2 orange

2-3 Tbsps olive oil

Peel the oranges, break into segments and cut them in half. Place in a bowl and toss with the carrots, oil, cinnamon, orange juice, honey, salt & pepper. Sprinkle with mint leaves and serve.

SHERRY-GLAZED CARROTS

1 lb/500g carrots

1 Tbsp butter

3 Tbsps sherry

1 Tbsp honey

Juice of 1/2 lemon

2-3 slices fresh ginger, julienned

1/2 cup walnuts

Heat the oil in a frypan and sauté the walnuts. Slice the carrots diagonally and add to the frypan with the butter, honey, ginger and sherry. Stir well and cook until the carrots are tender, about 5 minutes. Squeeze the lemon juice over just before serving.

CAULIFLOWER IN GREEN ADOBE SAUCE

1 whole cauliflower

3 canned jalapeno chillies, seeded & chopped

3 chillies, seeded & chopped

1/2 onion, chopped

3-4 cloves garlic, chopped

6 outer leaves of Romaine lettuce

2-3 green tomatoes and/or 1 green pepper

1 small bunch coriander leaves

1 Tbsp butter

1/4 cup orange juice

Salt & pepper

Steam the cauliflower whole in a saucepan or wok for 8-10 minutes. Meanwhile blend the chillies, onion, garlic, lettuce, tomatoes, green pepper and coriander in a food processor. Melt the butter in a frypan and cook the mixture for 2-3 minutes. Add the orange juice, salt and pepper and pour over the drained cauliflower.

FLAMBÉED CHERRY TOMATOES

2 cups cherry tomatoes

1 onion, cut in chunks

3 Tbsps brandy

Salt & pepper

1 tsp oregano

2 Tbsps olive oil

Heat the oil in a frypan and stir in the onions. Cook until browning but still crisp. Add the tomatoes and stir. Pour in the brandy and FLAMBÉ ! Add salt & pepper and serve.

LIMA BEANS WITH CARROT SHREDS

3 carrots, shredded
1 packet frozen lima beans
1 tsp tarragon
2 Tbsps yoghurt
1 Tbsp butter
Salt & pepper

Melt the butter in a frypan and sauté the lima beans quickly. Add the shredded carrot, tarragon, salt and pepper, cover and cook for 3 minutes. Stir in the yoghurt and serve. If you want to spice it up a little, add some hot pepper, or ground cumin or curry powder.

NASTURTIUM, SHRIMP & WATERCRESS SALAD

1 bunch watercress, washed
Fresh, peeled shrimp or 1 can shrimp
Nasturtium petals or any edible flowers (organically grown)
2 Tbsps olive oil
Juice of 1/2 lemon
Salt & pepper

Toss the watercress with olive oil, lemon juice, pepper and salt. Toss in the shrimp and garnish with flowers.

FAGIOLI ALL'UCCELLOTTO

1 can white beans, drained
3 Tbsps olive oil
1/2 tsp dried sage or a sprig of fresh
2 cloves garlic
3 ripe tomatoes, chopped
Pepper & salt

Heat the oil and put in the tomatoes, sage and lots of freshly ground black pepper. When the mixture is thick and syrupy, add the beans, salt and garlic. Heat through thoroughly and serve garnished with fresh sage.

KALE

2 Tbsps butter
Large bunch of kale, chopped
1/2 tsp salt
2 Tbsps buttermilk
1/2 cup oatmeal

In a dry frypan, gently toss the oatmeal until lightly browned and toasted, about 5-7 minutes. Melt the butter in a pan and add the kale. Sprinkle with salt and toss well. Pour in the buttermilk, cover and cook for 4 minutes. Sprinkle with toasted oatmeal.

BRAISED ONIONS IN WHISKEY

1 onion, sliced
1 Tbsp butter
2 Tbsps whiskey
Salt & pepper

Melt the butter in a frypan and sweat the onion. Sprinkle with salt and pepper, pour in the whiskey, cover and cook until tender.

'HOPPIN' JOHN (A Southern New Years Eve dish)

1 can black eyed peas
1/2 medium onion, chopped fine
3 stalks celery
2 cloves garlic, chopped fine
1 bunch parsley, chopped
1 Tbsp Dijon mustard
1/2 cup olive oil
3 Tbsp red wine vinegar
Salt & pepper

Drain and rinse the peas and place in a salad bowl. Chop the celery and mix into the peas with the rest of the ingredients. The traditional way is then to toss it all together with the hands and to hide a silver dime or quarter in the middle. Whoever finds it gets good luck for the rest of the year (if he doesn't get a dentist's bill !)

RAW VEGETABLES SERVED WITH OLIVE OIL

Arrange some fresh vegetables on a platter and serve with a dip of olive oil and balsamic vinegar. The best olive oil to use is the Cold Pressed, Extra Virgin Olive Oil.

STUFFED PEPPERS

4 peppers
1 cup breadcrumbs
1 onion, finely chopped
1 stick celery, finely chopped
1/3 cup sultanas
1/3 cup chopped dates
1/3 cup parsley, chopped
1 glass white wine
1 cup chopped, cooked turkey
1 Tbsp butter
Salt & pepper
1/2 cup grated, cheddar cheese

Blanch peppers in boiling water for 3 minutes and cut lengthwise into halves. Meanwhile in frypan, heat the butter and cook the onion, celery, breadcrumbs, sultanas, parsley and dates. Pour in the wine and stir well. Stuff the peppers with this mixture and lay the peppers in a greased baking dish, sprinkle with cheese and bake in a 400F/200C oven for 20-25 minutes.

PEANUT & CORIANDER SALAD

2 Tbsp oil
1/2 cup raw peanuts
1 cake firm tofu
1 bunch cilantro
1 1/2 Tbsp light soy sauce
1 tsp pepper
1/2 tsp sugar
2 Tbsp sesame oil
Bunch green onions, cut into thirds
5-6 whole fresh chillies or 1/2 tsp chilli flakes

Fry the peanuts and chillies in 1 Tbsp hot oil. Remove the nuts when browned. Cut the tofu into 1/8ths and fry both sides until brown. Stir in the onions, soy sauce, pepper, sugar and sesame oil until everything is well coated. Chop the cilantro leaves fairly coarse and stir in at the last minute. Serve on a bed of lettuce with the peanuts sprinkled on top. Decorate with chopped cilantro.

"EMIR'S PEARLS"

2 oranges, sliced
1/2 cup black olives, pitted
1/2 cup small onions
4 cloves garlic
1 tsp pepper
2 Tbsps sugar
2 Tbsps water
2 slices fresh ginger
2 Tbsps oil
1 Tbsp vinegar
Chopped cilantro or parsley

Peel the baby onions by blanching quickly in boiling water and then removing the skins. Boil the sugar, water, oil, ginger and garlic and drop in the onions. Cook until tender, about 5-10 minutes and add the vinegar at the last minute. Arrange the orange slices, black olives and onions in a bowl or plate and pour over some of the onion cooking liquid. Garnish with chopped cilantro or parsley.

PEAR & POTATO PURÉE

5-6 potatoes, cooked
2 pears, cooked or 1 can pears
2 Tbsps butter
Salt and pepper
Zest of 1/2 lime

Mash the hot potatoes and pears (warmed if necessary) together with the butter, seasoning and lime zest. Serve hot.

TAN TAN CABBAGE

1 small cabbage
3 cloves garlic

| 1/2 tsp salt |
| 2-3 Tbsps oil |
| 1 tsp pepper |
| 1/2 tsp cayenne pepper |
| 2 Tbsps peanut butter |
| 1/2 cup hot water |
| 1 tsp curry powder |
| Juice of 1/2 lemon |
| Zest of 1 lemon |

Chop the garlic and salt together. Quarter the cabbage, cut out the core and slice thin. Stirfry for 3 minutes, tossing continuously, until the cabbage has wilted. Add the garlic, salt, pepper, curry powder and cayenne pepper. Stir in the peanut butter, hot water and lemon juice, make sure everything is well mixed and serve hot decorated with thin strips of lemon zest.

POOR MAN'S LEEKS

| 10 small leeks |
| 3 hard-boiled eggs |

Wash and halve the leeks lengthwise. Steam in a little water, 1 Tbsp butter and 1/2 tsp salt for 2-3 minutes or until just tender. Cool. Cover with sauce.

SAUCE FOR LEEKS

| 6 green onions, chopped |
| 2 Tbsps chopped parsley |
| 1/2 tsp tarragon |
| 1/2 tsp thyme |
| 1/2 tsp paprika |
| 3 Tbsps red wine vinegar |
| 1/2 cup olive oil |
| 1/2 tsp salt |
| 1 tsp pepper |

Put all the sauce ingredients into an empty jar and shake well. Pour over the leeks, decorate with chopped hard-boiled eggs and some more chopped parsley. Serve chilled.

LEEKS IN RED WINE

| 8 small leeks, washed, trimmed & halved lengthwise |
| 1 Tbsp butter |
| 1 glass red wine |
| 1/2 tsp salt |
| 1 tsp pepper |
| 1/2 tsp sugar |

Heat the oil in a large frypan, lay in the whole leeks side by side and sprinkle with salt, pepper and sugar. Brown them, pour on the wine and bubble for a few minutes. Cover the pan and cook until tender, adding more wine if needed. Serve garnished with chopped parsley.

BOILED RADISHES

Top & tail a bunch of radishes and place in some boiling, salted water for 5-10 minutes, or until they're tender but still crisp. Add a tsp of vinegar or lemon juice to help retain the colour.

TURKISH FRIED CARROTS

4-5 carrots, peeled & sliced diagonally
Salt & pepper
2 Tbsps flour
2 Tbsps olive oil
1 cup yoghurt
Chopped mint and/or caraway seeds

Mix some salt and pepper in the flour and toss the carrot slices in this seasoned flour. Heat the oil in a frypan and fry the carrots over medium heat until seared and brown. Pour in the yoghurt, stir and serve on a warm plate. Garnish with mint, caraway seeds and, if available, pomegranate seeds.

HASHED ONIONS

3 large onions, peeled & chopped
1/2-1 cup milk
2 Tbsps butter
1/4-1/2 cup cream
1/2 tsp salt
1 tsp pepper
1/2 tsp nutmeg

Heat the 1/2 cup of milk in a frypan and add the onions, salt and pepper. Stir well and simmer for 10 minutes or until tender, adding more milk if necessary. Drain off the excess milk and add the butter, cream and nutmeg. Stir gently for a further 5 minutes until thick and creamy and serve hot.

BROCCOLI LORENZO

Heat 2 Tbsps oil in a frypan. Wash some broccoli, break into florets and sauté in the oil with 1/2 tsp salt. Toss well and pour in 1 glass of red wine and the segments of 1 mandarin. Cover tightly with a lid and cook over high heat for 3-4 minutes.

TUNISIAN PEPPER SALAD

2 red, bell peppers, diced
1 jalapeno pepper, finely chopped
4 garlic cloves, chopped
1/2 cup chopped, dried dates
1/2 cup chopped, dried apricots
1 tsp ground coriander
Juice of 1 lemon
2 Tbsps olive oil
Salt & pepper
Shredded leaves of 1/2 lettuce

Mix all the above ingredients together, chill and serve in a hollowed out half of melon.

BLACK-EYED PEA SALAD

1 can black-eyed peas
2 large tomatoes, chopped
4 small, Thai red peppers
1/2 onion, finely chopped
Handful of torn, fresh spinach leaves
Handful of chopped, fresh parsley or coriander
Juice of 1/2 lemon
Juice of 1/2 orange
1 clove garlic, chopped fine
1/2 cup yoghurt
1 tsp ground cumin
1/2 tsp salt
1 tsp pepper
3 Tbsps olive oil

Toss together the peas, onion, garlic, parsley, hot peppers and tomatoes. In a small bowl mix the lemon and orange juice, cumin, oil, salt and pepper and pour over the peas. Toss well, add the spinach leaves, coriander or parsley, top with the yoghurt and serve garnished with the segments of a mandarin orange.

GINGERED BEETS AND BRUSSEL SPROUTS

3 cups brussel sprouts, cleaned & trimmed
2 cooked & peeled beets or 1 can beets
2 Tbsps oil
2 slices fresh ginger, grated
1/2 glass red wine
Juice of 1/2 orange
Salt & pepper

Heat the oil in a frypan and sauté the sprouts and ginger, sprinkling the sprouts with salt to help keep them green. Slice the beets and add to the pan along with red wine. Sauté about 3-4 minutes, add the pepper, squeeze in the orange juice and stir for 1-2 minutes. Serve hot.

CHRISTMAS BRUSSEL SPROUTS

1lb/500g chestnuts
1lb/500g potatoes, cooked
4 Tbsps butter
1/4 cup cream
1 tsp salt
1 tsp pepper
2 egg yolks
1lb/500g mushrooms
1/2 cup white wine
1lb/500g brussel sprouts, trimmed
1/2 tsp aniseed
1 cup chopped parsley

Slit the sides of the chestnuts and boil for 20 minutes. Cool and peel. Mash the potatoes with 2 Tbsps butter, egg yolks, cream, salt, pepper and half the chestnuts. Heat the oil in a frypan and sauté the mushrooms. Add the wine, aniseed and salt and stir in the sprouts and the other half of chestnuts. Toss all together and cook for 2 minutes. Tip out onto a plate and arrange the mashed potato around the edges.

POTATO, STILTON & BEETROOT SALAD

1/2 lb/250g cooked potatoes
1 wedge stilton cheese
1 can small, whole beets
2 Tbsps olive oil
1 Tbsp pepper

Dice the potatoes and put in a bowl. Crumble the stilton and mix with the potatoes. Add the drained beets and arrange on lettuce leaves. Pour over the oil and sprinkle with pepper.

FRIED CUCUMBERS

1 cucumber, cut into small logs
Cracker crumbs
2 Tbsps oil
1/2 tsp cayenne pepper
1 egg, beaten

Dip the cucumber pieces in the beaten egg and roll in cracker crumbs mixed with cayenne pepper. Fry in the hot oil until golden brown and pile onto a platter. Serve hot.

DESSERTS & DRINKS

ORANGE DESSERT

Cut an orange in half and cut the round end off each half. With a small sharp knife cut out the inside meat of the orange and put the end bit into the inside of the empty shell. Cut up the orange meat and pile into the shell. Top with a grape and serve on a small plate.

ICED MUFFINS

4 Tbsps cream cheese
1 cup confectioner's sugar
1 tsp oil

Mix all the ingredients together until they form a smooth paste or icing. Add colouring if you wish. Ice any muffins and decorate.

APPLES & YOGHURT

2 Tbsps sesame seeds - lightly browned in pan
4 Tbsps yoghurt
1 apple - cored & cut into eighths
Maple syrup

Spoon the yoghurt into 2 bowls and arrange the apple slices around the edges. Sprinkle over the sesame seeds and pour a little maple syrup over the top.

APPLES BRETON STYLE

1 tsp butter
1 apple - cored & cut into 1/2" thick slices
1 Tbsp brown sugar
Juice of 1/2 lemon
1 tsp cinnamon
2 Tbsps rye or bourbon

Melt the butter in a frypan and lay in the apple rings. Add the brown sugar and lemon juice and cook until lightly browned and the sugar caramelized. Sprinkle with cinnamon and pour in the rye or bourbon, set light and FLAMBÉ!

BAKED APPLES

Cut a line around the middle of the apple and 4 more lines down from the top to the middle and core it. Stuff the apple with a mixture of chopped walnuts, raisins, some brown sugar and a little rye or bourbon if wished. Cook, covered, in microwave for 5 minutes.

FRIED EGGS

1 can peach halves
Crème fraîche

⤴ CRÈME FRAÎCHE

To make crème fraîche pour some cream into a medium sized jar (about 500 ml) and stir in 2 Tbsps buttermilk. Put the lid on loosely and leave UNTOUCHED at room temperature for 24 hours. It will be thick, and can now be kept in the refrigerator for a week or two, in a jar with a lid.

Spoon some crème fraîche onto a plate. Carefully place a peach half on top, sprinkle some ground ginger over and serve as a FRIED EGG!

For a Peach Sauce, blend some peaches with a little sherry and serve over the top of ice cream.

ATHOLL BROSE

1 cup cream - whipped
2 Tbsps liquid honey
2 Tbsps scotch whiskey or brandy
2 Tbsps granola or toasted oatmeal

Stir together the honey and whiskey and fold into the whipped cream. Add the granola and gently stir. Place some strawberries or raspberries into the bottom of a tall glass and pile the cream mixture on top. Decorate with a small handful of granola and serve.

WATERMELON & LIME

Cut the watermelon into slices and arrange on a plate with fresh lime slices.

RHUBARB & GINGER

1 bunch rhubarb
2 tsps butter
1" piece ginger - grated
1 Tbsp brown sugar
Juice of 1/2 lemon

Melt the butter in a saucepan. Cut off and discard the green ends of the rhubarb and cut into bite-sized pieces. Stir in the ginger and sugar with the melted butter, add the rhubarb pieces and stir. Squeeze the juice of 1/2 lemon in, put the lid on and cook for 3 minutes. Serve with some fresh mint leaves.

CRÊPES WITH VODKA & BLACK CHERRIES

4 eggs
1/2 cup flour
2 Tbsps sugar
1 cup beer
2 Tbsps melted butter

Whisk the eggs in a large bowl and stir in the flour and sugar. Whisk in the beer, add the melted butter and allow to stand for 30 minutes.

Heat up a frypan over medium heat and, using a small ladle, pour in the batter, tipping it round the pan. Loosen the edges and toss. Slide the crêpe onto a plate, pour some sauce over the top and fold over. Serve with whipped cream or ice cream and extra black cherries.

1 cup black cherries
1 tsp butter
1 Tbsp sugar
2 Tbsps vodka

Melt the butter in a small pan and tip in the black cherries. Stir in the sugar and pour in the vodka. Set light and flambé if you wish. Allow to sit.

FRENCH TOAST

Take the crêpe batter as above and add a little more sugar and milk. Dip slices of bread into the batter and fry in a pan. Brown each side and serve with fresh fruit and cream.

MANGO DESSERT

Hold a ripe mango on the narrow side and cut down 1/4" from the centre on each side to produce 2 slices. With a small knife cut the flesh into cubes keeping the flesh intact with the skin and turn inside out. Place on a plate and decorate with a strawberry.

CHOCOLATE SAUCE

3/4 cup apple juice
3/4 cup brown sugar
1/3 cup cocoa powder
2 tsps instant coffee
2 Tbsps butter
2 Tbsps cold cream or whipped cream

Heat the apple juice, brown sugar, cocoa powder and coffee in a saucepan. Bring to boiling point and then whisk in the butter. When melted and thickened, stir in the cold cream and serve over peeled pears garnished with whipped cream, nuts and cherries.

SPACESHIP ORANGES

1 orange
Red & green grapes
ice cream

Cut off one end of the orange and with a small knife cut round the inside shell and scoop out the flesh. Insert toothpicks into the shell at a slight angle and press a red or a green grape on each one (or you could use strawberries or banana chunks). Fill the middle with some coloured ice cream, replace the lid and serve.

STUFFED CANNELLONI DESSERT

Cannelloni shells (2 per person)
Ricotta cheese
1 can peaches
Cointreau or grappa or any orange liqueur

Boil the cannelloni shells for 12 minutes. Remove and when cooled, slit up the middle, open out and stuff with about 1 Tbsp ricotta cheese. Roll up and arrange them on a plate. Blend 2 peaches (with some juice) and about 1 Tbsp cointreau in a blender until smooth and pour this sauce over the stuffed cannelloni. Serve cold.

SWEET OMELETTE WITH RASPBERRIES

2 egg yolks - beaten
2 tsp sugar
2 egg whites - stiffly beaten
1 tsp butter
Raspberries

Mix the egg yolks and sugar and gently fold in the egg whites with a metal spoon. Melt the butter in a small frypan and pour in the eggs. Cook over high heat for a few minutes until set, slide onto a plate, spoon some raspberries into the middle and fold over. Serve immediately sprinkled with sugar.

JAM BUTTY, A North Country Childrens' Delight

Melt 1 tsp butter in a frypan. Butter 2 thick slices of bread, spread with some jam and put the 2 pieces together. Beat 1 egg in a bowl with 1 tsp sugar, dip the jam butty in the egg and fry until crisp and brown on each side. Serve sprinkled with sugar and some cream.

CHOCOLATE DUBARRY

1 Tbsp cocoa powder
1 Tbsp sugar
1/2 cup whipping cream

Whip the cream until stiff and fold in the cocoa powder and sugar. Spoon into ramekin dishes (or pretty little ovenproof bowls) and bake in a 400 F/200 C oven for 5-8 minutes.

RICE PUDDING WITH SULTANAS

1 cup rice
3 cups milk (or 1/2 milk + 1/2 cream)
1 egg - optional
2 Tbsps sugar
1/2 cup sultanas
2 drops vanilla extract
1/2 tsp nutmeg
1/2 tsp cinnamon
Freshly ground pepper
1 Tbsp brandy - optional

Put the rice, milk, egg (if using) and sugar into a saucepan and heat up gently. Pour boiling water over the sultanas and allow to sit for a few minutes. Add the vanilla, nutmeg, cinnamon and pepper to the saucepan and stir. Strain the sultanas and add to the rice and pour into a greased baking dish. Place in a 325 F/170 C oven and cook for 30-40 minutes. Sprinkle the top with slivered almonds and cook for a few more minutes. Serve.

ZABAGLIONE

3 eggs
2 Tbsps sugar
4 Tbsps sherry or marsala

Beat the eggs until frothy and then stir in the sugar and sherry. Whisk in a double boiler or in a saucepan raised slightly away from the heat. Whisk for about 3-5 minutes or until it thickens and serve immediately in a glass or bowl.

PEARS IN RED WINE

2 cups red wine
1 Tbsp sugar
1 tsp oregano
2 pears - peeled, cored and halved

Bring the red wine, sugar and oregano to a boil and carefully place the pear halves in. Put the lid on and simmer over a medium heat for 15 minutes. Lift out the pears onto a plate and serve with ice cream. If you wish you can boil down the red wine to make a syrup and pour this over the pears.

STUFFED FIGS

Plunge the dried figs into boiling water for 2 minutes to soften them up. Slit down the middle of each fig, without cutting them completely in half. Poke in about 4 almonds and fold up. Roll each one in grated coconut and arrange on a plate with some more coconut scattered over the top.

PÂTHE À CHOUX OR DOUGHNUTS

1 cup water
4 Tbsps butter
1 cup flour
4 eggs
Oil for deep frying
Sugar

Bring the water almost to the boil, stir in the butter with a wooden spoon then add the flour all in one go. Remove from the heat and quickly stir in until the dough comes away from the edge of the pan in a ball. Beat in the eggs one at a time until the dough is smooth and shiny. Heat 1" oil in a deep-sided pan to about 350 F/180 C and slide teaspoonfuls of dough into the hot oil. When brown and crispy all over, remove with a slotted spoon and roll in sugar. Serve piled on a plate and scatter some sugar over the top.

CRÊPES

4 eggs
1 cup flour
1 Tbsp sugar
Milk
1 Tbsp melted butter

Break the eggs into a bowl and beat well. Whisk in the flour and sugar and enough milk to make a consistency of thin cream. Whisk in the melted butter. Heat a frypan over medium heat and ladle in some batter tipping it round the pan. Toss. Slide onto a plate, sprinkle with sugar and roll up. Squeeze a little lemon juice over, sprinkle with some more sugar and serve.

ROMANTIC PEARS

Cut out a cardboard heart shape and poke a pin through each end. Lay on a plate, with the heads of the pins underneath and sprinkle some icing sugar over the top. Carefully lift up the heart using the two pins and place a peeled pear half in the middle. Sprinkle with lemon juice to prevent browning and grate some chocolate over the top.

YOGHURT HOTCAKES

3 eggs
1 cup flour
3/4 cup yoghurt
2 Tbsps sugar
1 heaped tsp baking powder
Milk
3 Tbsps oil

Break the eggs into a bowl and beat until frothy. Whisk in the flour, then the sugar, yoghurt, salt, oil and baking powder. Heat up a frypan and ladle in enough batter to almost cover the bottom of the pan. Brown on both sides and serve with more yoghurt and fresh fruit.

MARBLED YOGHURT

Mix equal parts of yoghurt and cream together and pour into a small glass bowl. Sprinkle some brown sugar over the top and leave in the fridge for at least 4 hours or overnight.

BOUGATSA

1 Tbsp orange zest - julienned
Juice of 1 orange
2 Tbsps liquid honey
1 tsp oregano
Shredded wheat

Cut the shredded wheat into 4 pieces, using a sharp knife and arrange on a plate. Bring the orange zest, orange juice, honey and oregano to a boil, stir well and pour over the shredded wheat. Leave for 5 minutes to marinate and serve with whipped cream or yoghurt.

BANANAS & CREAM

Mash 2 bananas with lemon juice and 1 tsp sugar. Spoon onto a plate and arrange some blueberries around the edge. Top with whipped cream and sprinkle with cinnamon.

BAKED APPLES & CHEESE

Halve an apple across the middle, slice the ends off and remove the core. Fill the cavity with some brown sugar and grated cheese and bake in a 450 F/230 C oven for 7 minutes. Serve bubbling hot.

BREAD & BUTTER PUDDING

6-8 slices of stale bread
3/4 cup sultanas
3/4 cup currants
3 Tbsps brown sugar
4 eggs
1 cup cream
1 tsp grated nutmeg

Butter the slices of bread and cover the bottom of a greased casserole dish with a single layer, buttered side down. Sprinkle with sultanas and currants and cover with another layer of bread. Sprinkle over 2 Tbsps brown sugar, some more sultanas and currants and another layer of bread. Lightly beat the eggs with the cream and nutmeg and pour over the bread. Press down to make sure everything is well soaked. Sprinkle a little more sugar over the top and bake in a 375 F/190 C oven for 30 minutes, until top is brown and crusty.

STRAWBERRIES & QUARK

Arrange on a plate mounds of quark, yoghurt or sour cream (or all three), some brown sugar and some fresh strawberries. Dip the strawberries into the quark and then into the brown sugar and EAT!

CLAFOUTI

2 eggs
2 Tbsps sugar
1 cup flour
1 cup milk
2 cans black cherries - strained (or any other fruit)

Break the eggs into a bowl and beat with the sugar, flour and milk to make a smooth batter. Put the cherries into a greased baking dish and pour over the batter. Bake in a pre-heated 350 F/180 C oven for 30 minutes. Serve with whipped cream or a light sprinkling of sugar.

QUATTRO STAGIONE (Dessert Or Kids Pizza)

Quick pizza one (see above)
1 Tbsp safflower oil
1 banana
Chocolate chips
Sultanas
Chopped pineapple

Heat the oil in a frypan and lay in the dough. Place chopped banana on one quarter, chocolate chips on another quarter, sultanas on another and chopped pineapple on another. Cook as for Quick Pizza One and serve with some sugar, orange juice or cream.

CUCUMBER & STRAWBERRIES

1 cucumber
Fresh strawberries
Freshly ground pepper
2-3 Tbsps yoghurt

Cut the cucumber into wedge-shaped slices and chop. Arrange on a plate with the fresh strawberries. Grind a generous amount of pepper over the top and toss with the yoghurt.

APPLE CRUMBLE

4-5 apples
1 1/2 cups granola
3/4 cup brown sugar
1 Tbsp butter

Peel, core and slice the apples and put them in water and lemon juice to stop them browning. Mix together the granola, half the sugar and the butter. Lay the apple slices in the bottom of a greased baking dish and sprinkle with some brown sugar. Top with the granola mixture and the rest of the sugar. Bake in 375 F/190 C oven for 25-30 minutes. Beat together equal parts of yoghurt and whipping cream and serve with the crumble.

MANGO & YOGHURT

2 mangoes
1/2 lime
3-4 Tbsps yoghurt

Slice the mangoes and scoop out the flesh into a food processor or blender. Add the lime juice and yoghurt and blend until smooth and creamy. Serve in glass bowls.

FRUIT SOUP

Halve a melon and cut a thin slice from the bottom of each half to enable them to stand. Scoop out the flesh (discarding the seeds) and blend in the food processor or blender with some fresh mint, 1 Tbsp sugar, the juice of a lemon and 3/4 cup of white wine. When the soup is smooth and frothy, pour into the melon halves and sprinkle with some freshly ground pepper.

MACERATED FRUIT

Sprinkle 1 Tbsp brown sugar over 1/2 lb of fresh strawberries and marinate in 3/4 cup of red wine for 2 hours. Serve in glass bowls with whipped cream.

MARBLED PRUNES & YOGHURT

Plump up some prunes in boiling water and lemon zest for 2 minutes. Strain and purée in a blender or food processor. Stir into yoghurt (or sour cream) until you have a marbled effect. Garnish with slivered almonds and cocoa powder.

MELON & GRAPES

Cut a thin slice off the bottom of a melon to enable it to stand upright. Cut out a large wedge-shaped slice and spoon out the seeds. Fill the inside with green and black grapes and pour over some white wine. Serve cold.

COTTAGE CHEESE & COFFEE

Place spoonfuls of cottage cheese onto a plate and sprinkle sugar and freshly ground coffee (or instant coffee) over the top. Decorate and serve.

FLAMBÉED BANANAS

2 bananas
1 Tbsp butter
1 Tbsp brown sugar
1/2 tsp cinnamon
2-4 Tbsps brandy

Peel the bananas, cut in half crosswise and then half again lengthwise. Melt the butter in a frypan and immediately lay in the bananas. Cook for 1 minute, turning once, until slightly coloured. Add the brown sugar and cinnamon, pour in the brandy and set alight.

TREASURE WINTER CUSTARD

2 eggs
1 cup milk
3 cloves
3 allspice berries
1 Tbsp sugar
1/2 tsp cinnamon
3/4 cup candied fruit (mixed peel) or any combination of chopped apricots, prunes, figs, dates, peaches or pears

Beat the eggs in a bowl with the sugar and cinnamon. Warm the milk with the cloves and allspice berries (don't boil it). Stir the milk into the eggs, divide the fruits among 6 small ramekins and pour the milk and egg mixture over the top. Steam for 20 minutes. They can also be cooked in a pan of water in the oven. Turn out when cool, and serve with chopped crystallized ginger. You can also add 1 Tbsp cooked rice to each small ramekin if wished (this is the "8th treasure!").

PUDING DE PATATA (Sweet Minorcan Potato Cake)

2 large potatoes, peeled & cooked
1/2 tsp pepper
1/2 tsp cinnamon
3 eggs, separated
3/4 cup sugar
Zest of 1 lemon
1/2 cup sliced almonds
1 Tbsp butter

Mash the potatoes with a little butter, the pepper and cinnamon until smooth. Beat the egg whites until stiff. Thoroughly mix the potatoes, egg yolks, sugar and the lemon zest. Fold in the egg whites and pour into a small, oiled baking dish. Pat smooth and bake for 20 minutes, or until a toothpick in the middle comes out clean, in a 350F/180C oven. Cool, turn out onto a serving dish and sprinkle with a little more sugar and the almonds that have been lightly sautéed in butter.

PRINCESS DI'S NANNY'S FAVE PUDDING

1 lb/500g berries
1 cup flour
1 egg
2 Tbsps sugar
1 Tbsp baking powder
Milk to make up to 1 cup

Beat the egg lightly and add the sugar. Pour in the milk to make up to 1 cup and mix into the flour and baking powder. Put 1 lb fresh berries, or 1 can berries, or 1 packet frozen berries into a large saucepan, add the batter and bring to a boil. Turn down the heat to medium and simmer for about 15 minutes with the lid on. Serve with fresh cream and sprinkled with sugar.

STRAWBERRIES & PEPPER

Place spoonfuls of sour cream on a plate and top each mound with a fresh strawberry. Grind some fresh pepper over the top and serve.

STRAWBERRY CAKE

Whipped cream
Sponge cake
Sugar
Cointreau
Fresh strawberries

Slice a sponge cake into 3 long layers. Lay the first layer on a plate or tray and spoon on some whipped cream. Sprinkle with sugar and cointreau and repeat with the other layers of cake. Finally cover with whipped cream and decorate with the strawberries. Serve.

SWEET POTATO PUFFS

2 cups cooked sweet potatoes
1 egg white - stiffly beaten
1 egg yolk
1 banana
2 Tbsps oil or melted butter
1 tsp salt
3-4 Tbsps cream

Blend the sweet potatoes, banana, egg yolk, salt and cream until smooth in a food processor or blender. Pour into a bowl and fold in the egg white with a metal spoon. Put spoonfuls of the mixture onto a greased baking sheet and bake in a preheated 500 F/250 C oven for 6-8 minutes. Serve sprinkled with a little sugar and grated nutmeg.

STRAWBERRY OR RASPBERRY FOOL

2 cups strawberries or raspberries, slightly mashed or sliced.
1 cup whipping cream
Sugar - optional

Whip the cream until stiff and beat the berries into the cream. Add some sugar if preferred and spoon into glass bowls. Decorate.

BANANAS AU CHOCOLAT

2 bananas - peeled & quartered lengthwise
1 tsp butter
1 Tbsp brown sugar
2 pieces unsweetened or semi-sweet chocolate

Melt the butter in a frypan and gently lay in the bananas. Sprinkle over the brown sugar and lay the grated or slivered chocolate on top of the bananas. Put the lid on and cook for about 2 minutes. Serve with ice cream, crème fraîche or cream.

FRIED NOODLES & HONEY

1 Tbsp orange zest - cut in thin strips
1 Tbsp olive oil or butter
3-4 Tbsps liquid honey
2 Tbsps scotch whiskey (or grappa)
Juice of 1/2 lemon
2 shakes of cayenne pepper
Leftover cold pasta, such as linguine

Fry spoonfuls of cold pasta in the oil, tossing in the pan to brown both sides. Make the sauce by heating the honey, orange zest, scotch, lemon juice and cayenne pepper. Bring to the boil, stir and drizzle the sauce over the pancakes. Serve either hot or cold.

PASTELLA

1 cup beer (or water)
Flour (appx. 1/2 - 3/4 cup)
1 apple - cut into wedges
Oil for deep frying

Pour the beer into a bowl. Sprinkle in the flour beating it with a fork until the mixture is as thick as light cream. Heat about 1/2" oil in a saucepan. Dip the apple wedges into the batter and then drop into the hot oil. When light brown and puffed up, about 1-2 minutes, remove to a plate and dust with a little confectioner's sugar.

SLICED ORANGES

1 orange - thinly sliced
Mint leaves
Cointreau

Cut halfway through each orange slice. Arrange the slices on a small plate. Place a mint leaf in each cut and drizzle the cointreau over.

ARROZ DOCE

3 Tbsps arborio, or short-grain, rice
2 cups light cream
3 Tbsps sugar
3 Tbsps butter
Zest of a lemon - julienned
1 tsp cinnamon

Grease a baking dish and pour in the rice, cream, sugar, butter and lemon zest. Mix gently and bake in a 250 F /130 C oven for 45 minutes - 2 hours. Sprinkle with cinnamon and serve, hot or cold.

ORANGE SAUCE & ICE CREAM

Heat 2 Tbsps marmalade and 2 Tbsps whiskey in a small pan. Stir well and when bubbling remove from heat and allow to cool a little. Serve over ice cream and garnish with strips of orange zest.

MARMALADE SPONGE

1/4 cup butter
1/4 cup flour
1/4 cup sugar
1 Tbsp baking powder
1 egg
1/2 cup milk or water
2 Tbsps marmalade

Mix together the butter, flour, sugar and baking powder in a bowl. Beat the egg into the milk or water and add to the flour. Put 2 Tbsps marmalade into the bottom of a greased bowl and pour the batter on top. Microwave at power 8 for 6 minutes. Remove and turn out onto a plate.

LEMON & MINT GRANITA

2-3 trays ice-cubes
Juice of 2 lemons
2 Tbsps sugar
1 bunch fresh mint
1 Tbsp sherry or brandy

Crush all the above ingredients together in a food processor and serve immediately decorated with a fresh mint leaf.

ORANGE & CHOCOLATE

Peel an orange and break into segments. Arrange the segments on a plate and sprinkle with shaved chocolate.

BANANA FRITTERS & COCONUT MILK

2 bananas
1 egg yolk
1/4 cup flour
Milk
1 can coconut milk
Oil for deep frying

Whisk the egg yolk and flour together in a bowl. Heat the oil in a high-sided saucepan. Peel the bananas and halve them crosswise, then again lengthwise. Dip them in the batter and then into the hot oil for 1-2 minutes. Remove with a slotted spoon and sprinkle them with sugar. Mix the can of coconut milk well and pour some onto a plate. Arrange the banana fritters on top and serve.

CHOCOLATE FLOWER-COVERED FROZEN BANANAS

Cut a peeled banana into chunks, place on a plate and freeze for at least 1 hour.

Melt in a double boiler:
6 Tbsps chocolate,
2 Tbsps butter,
1/2 cup brown sugar
1/3 cup cream

Pierce the frozen banana chunks with toothpicks and dip into the hot chocolate sauce. Roll immediately, before the sauce hardens, in the petals of edible flowers, and serve immediately.

GREEK STYLE COUNTRY BOUGATSA

Halve the pita bread and open up each half into a pocket. Fill with crumbled feta cheese, a good handful of well-rubbed oregano and 1 Tbsp liquid honey. Broil in a toaster oven for 5-8 minutes or barbecue with the lid down.

STRAWBERRIES & MANGO

1 mango
2 cups strawberries
Yoghurt
Grated chocolate

Slice the sides off the mango. Score with a knife into squares. Turn inside out and slide the cubes off the skin with a knife. Pour some yoghurt onto a plate and arrange the mango cubes and strawberries on top. Sprinkle with grated chocolate and serve.

VOL AU VENTS

Cook some frozen vol au vents cases and fill with a mixture of chopped apricots, dates, toasted walnuts and feta cheese. Drizzle with honey and a little oregano.

APPLE CREAM

2 grated apples
Juice of half a lemon
1/2 cup grated coconut
2 Tbsps heavy cream or silken tofu

Mix together and allow to rest for up to 30 minutes. Serve garnished with orange curls.

GINGER SYLLABUB

1/4 cup ginger syrup (below) or ginger wine
1 tsp lemon zest, finely chopped
1/4 cup white sugar
2 Tbsp brandy
1 cup whipping cream
4 ginger biscuits
Finely chopped fresh ginger

Boil 1/2 cup water with sugar and 6 slices of fresh ginger until it has reduced to about 1/4 cup and slightly thickened. Strain and cool. Mix this syrup (or use ginger wine) with the lemon zest. Allow to cool then stir in the brandy. Whip the cream until very thick. Stir in the ginger mixture. Put biscuits in the bottom of four bowls or wine glasses. Spoon the syllabub on top. Decorate with stem ginger. Chill and serve.

POACHED NECTARINES

1 cup water or apple juice
1 cup white wine
1 cup sugar
3-4 slices of ginger, julienned
4 nectarines, quartered

Simmer the water, wine, sugar and ginger for 10 minutes. Add the nectarines and simmer for further 2-3 minutes. Serve warm in some liquid with crème fraîche/sour cream and some mint leaves.

FRUITS RAFRAICHIS SERVED IN HALF A MELON

Scoop out half a melon and fill with any fresh fruit you have, e.g. strawberries, kiwis, grapes and apples. Sprinkle with some lemon juice and a little sugar and pour over some cider.

PUFF PASTRY ZUCCHINIS

Roll out some puff pastry on a floured board and cut out zucchini shapes. Bake on a cookie sheet in a 400F/200C oven for about 6-8 minutes. Serve sprinkle with icing sugar and fresh or frozen raspberries.
Cut out heart-shaped puff pastry and bake for 10-15 minutes. Sprinkle with icing sugar and raspberries.

DESSERT CORN FRITTERS

1 fresh corn on the cob
2 Tbsps flour

2 eggs
1 tsp baking powder
1 tsp sugar

Mix all the ingredients together in a bowl or food processor and fry spoonfuls in butter or oil until browned on each side. Serve with any fresh or frozen fruit and some yoghurt or sour cream.

CUCUMBER/MINT/STRAWBERRY KEBABS

Peel & chop a cucumber. Thread chunks of cucumber, whole strawberries and fresh mint leaves onto a wooden skewer. Serve with sweetened yoghurt.

BLUEBERRY MUFFINS

1/2 cup fresh or frozen blueberries

Mix dry:

2 cups flour
1/3 cup sugar
1 tsp baking powder
1 tsp baking soda
1/2 tsp salt

Mix wet:

1/4 cup orange juice
2 Tbsp vegetable oil
1/2 cup yoghurt
1 egg

Mix the two together being careful not to overstir, and fold in 1/2 cup fresh or frozen blueberries. Spoon into lightly oiled muffin tins, sprinkle a little sugar over top and bake in a 400F/200C oven for 15-20 minutes. Take out of pans immediately and cool on racks. Makes 12 muffins.

BLUEBERRIES & GINGER

Mix some frozen blueberries & chopped, crystallized ginger pieces in a glass bowl. Top with yoghurt and mint leaves.

To freeze fresh blueberries, wash and place on a cookie sheet and put in the freezer. When each berry is solidly frozen, place in plastic bags and keep frozen.

FIG GRATIN

1 cup of halved fresh or dried figs (soak the dried figs first)
1/2 cup whipping cream
2 egg yolks
1 tsp honey
1 Tbsp sherry or white wine

Place the figs in a small ovenproof dish. Beat the whipping cream, egg yolks, honey and sherry together and pour over the figs. Broil for 3-4 minutes or until browned and bubbly.

BANANAS " BANGERS & MASH "

Peel bananas and halve. Roll in chocolate sauce, then crushed peanuts and serve around ice cream. Sprinkle with grated coconut and drizzle with honey or maple syrup.

BANANA SPLIT

Layer in a dessert bowl, 1 or 2 halved and peeled bananas, whipped cream, or ice cream and decorate with any of the following indulgences:chopped nuts, sprinkles, grated chocolate, maple syrup, jam, grated coconut and anything you wish. Do this once a year for your kids or for yourself.

PINEAPPLE WITH PORT

Put a slice of pineapple (fresh or canned) on a plate. Sprinkle with sugar and pour some port over the top.

FIG NUT FOOL

1 cup/225g dried figs
2 Tbsps rum
Juice of 1/2 a lemon
1 cup whipping cream
1 cup/100g walnuts

Chop the figs roughly and put in the food processor with rum, lemon and 1/2 cup water. Blend until smooth. Beat the whipping cream until stiff. Roast the walnuts on high heat for 4 minutes, rub the skins off and chop. Fold walnuts into the cream with the figs using a metal spoon.

QUICK SHERRY TRIFLE

for each person:

1 sponge finger
1 Tbsp sweet sherry
2 Tbsp whipped cream
1/2 tsp chopped hazelnuts
1 Tbsp jam

Break the biscuit into a glass bowl. Pour over the sherry. Put in the jam, top with the whipped cream and decorate with nuts. Leave to sit over dinner.

INSTANT BANANA ICE CREAM

Peel some bananas, cut into chunks and place on a baking tray. Freeze. Remove the frozen banana pieces and blend with cream or yoghurt, lemon juice and rum (optional). Serve sprinkled with shaved chocolate.

SWISS ROLL (Or Jelly Roll)

6 eggs
1/2 cup sugar
1 Tbsp flour
1/2 tsp baking powder
Jam

Separate the eggs and beat the yolks with the sugar until fluffy. Add the flour slowly while still beating. Whip egg whites until stiff and dry and fold into the yolks with a metal spoon. Bake in a shallow tin lined with waxed paper. Cook in 450F/220C oven for 10 minutes. Turn out onto another sheet of paper which has been dusted with sugar. Spread jam over and roll up quickly with the paper.

BANANA OMELETTE WITH APRICOT JAM

2 bananas
5 eggs
1 Tbsp butter
Sugar
Apricot Jam

Slice bananas and toss in granulated sugar. Melt butter in pan and caramelize bananas. Separate eggs and beat the yolks. Whisk the whites until firm. Fold yolks into the whites. Push the banana slices together into the centre of the pan and pour the egg mixture around them. When the top has set serve with a little warmed apricot jam as a sauce.

PEARS BRÛLÉE

1 fresh pear, halved or canned pears
Brown sugar

Slice the pear halves (not quite through) and fan out on a plate. Sprinkle with brown sugar and a squeeze of lemon juice and put under the broiler until bubbling. Garnish with chopped almonds.

PUMPKIN PUFFS

2 cups cooked pumpkin (or canned)
3/4 cup flour
1 Tbsp baking powder
1/2 cup sugar
1/2 tsp salt
3 eggs
1 Tbsp sugar & cinnamon
1 Tbsp finely chopped orange zest
Oil

Mix the flour, baking powder, sugar and salt together in a bowl. Beat the pumpkin and eggs and stir into the flour mixture. Heat enough oil in a high sided pan to come 1/3 of the way up. Drop teaspoons of batter in and fry until golden. Drain and sprinkle with sugar & cinnamon.

INSTANT MINCE PIES

Mix together any selection of chopped nuts, chopped figs, dates, dried apricots, orange zest, chopped glace fruit - it's your choice. Form them into small balls, roll them in grated coconut, flatten, and put a cherry in the middle. Hey presto... Instant mince pies !

RASPBERRY ALMOST CHARLOTTE

Blend 1 packet of frozen raspberries in a food processor or blender. Cut some day old bread into fingers and fry in butter until golden brown. Put some vanilla ice cream in middle of a plate, tumble the bread sticks over, drizzle the raspberry syrup over all and dust with dessicated coconut and/or sugar.

DRUNKEN WATERMELON

Marinate chunks of watermelon with 3 Tbsps brandy and 2 Tbsps of sugar. Serve in a glass bowl sprinkled with chocolate shavings.

CORN BREAD & WALNUT DESSERT

Quick sauté some walnuts in a little butter. Cut a slice of corn bread and lay on a dessert plate. Put 2 Tbsps yoghurt on top of the bread, drizzle over some maple syrup and top with the walnuts. Decorate with sliced apple and serve.

BEANS

There are no bean desserts, if you're going to give people dessert after a bean supper then it should look exotic. So, mix 1 can of drained lychees and some fresh black grapes together and pile into a glass bowl. Decorate with some fresh berries such as blueberries, red currants or any colour that you wish.

SLICED KIWIS & CHOCOLATE SAUCE

Kiwi fruit, peeled & sliced
2 large squares of baking chocolate
1 tsp butter
2 Tbsps whipping cream
1 tsp sugar (optional)
Yoghurt

Melt the chocolate, butter and cream in a double boiler or in the microwave for 1 minute at Power 5. Stir in the sugar, if using, and pour onto a plate. Lay the kiwi slices on top and decorate with some yoghurt or more whipping cream.

SHORTBREAD

1 cup butter
1/2 cup sugar
1 1/2 cups plain flour
Pinch of salt
1 can pear halves, drained or fresh pears, peeled & halved

Cream the butter, salt and sugar. Add the flour and pat into an oblong shape. Arrange the pears in a small ovenproof dish and place the shortbread on top. Prick with a fork and bake for 20-25 minutes in a 350F/180C oven.

PINEAPPLE & ORANGE SALAD WITH TOASTED ALMONDS

1 cup chopped pineapple
2 oranges, peeled and thinly sliced
1/4 cup/50g toasted almonds

Toss all together, allow to sit for 20 minutes and serve drizzled with rum and a little cream. Serve in a hollowed out pineapple.

BOURBON, PEARS, CREAM & TOASTED PECANS

1 fresh pear, peeled, cored and halved
1/3 cup whipping cream
2 Tbsps bourbon or whiskey
Toasted pecans

Heat the bourbon and cream in a frypan until slightly reduced and thickened. Pour onto a plate. Slice the pears, and arrange them fan-shaped on the pool of cream and bourbon and sprinkle with chopped, roasted pecans.

GRILLED PAPAYA

1 papaya, halved and seeded
1 Tbsp brown sugar
1/2 tsp cinnamon

Cut the papaya into lengths and lay on an ovenproof plate or dish. Sprinkle the sugar and cinnamon over and place under the broiler until hot and bubbling. Serve immediately with a squeeze of lemon or lime juice.

ORANGE & CARDAMON CAKE

2 oranges
3/4 cup flour
2 tsps baking powder
1/2 cup sugar
6 Tbsps olive oil
2 eggs
1 tsp ground cardamom

Grate the zest from the oranges and squeeze the juice. Mix and set aside. Sift the flour and baking powder into a bowl and mix in the sugar and cardamon. Beat the eggs, add the olive oil, orange juice and zest and stir into the dry ingredients. Turn into a greased cake or loaf pan and cook for 45-50 minutes at 350F/180C (or takes 20 minutes if you use smaller pans). Good warm or cold. Sprinkle with icing sugar.

CANDIED WALNUT HALVES

2 Tbsps sugar
1/2 cup/100g walnut halves
1 Tbsp oil
Pinch of cayenne pepper

Blanch the walnuts in boiling water, drain and toss with the sugar and cayenne pepper. Heat the oil in a frypan and fry the walnuts for 4-5 minutes over high heat until they are glistening. Don't darken them or else they will be bitter. Allow to cool and keep in airtight jar.

HAZELNUT FLAN & RASPBERRIES

1 cup hazelnuts
3 Tbsps liquid honey
Juice of a lemon
1 1/2/ cups/350g raspberries
1/4 cup brown sugar
2 cups whipping cream

Grind the hazelnuts in a food processor and add honey & lemon juice. Press the mixture into an 8"/20cm quiche or flan dish and chill. Whip the cream. Pat down the raspberries into the pie shell, sprinkle with the brown sugar and pile the whipped cream on top. Keep chilled.

HOT APRICOTS WITH GIN BUTTER

2 Tbsps butter
2 Tbsps gin
1 Tbsp sugar
1 Tbsp ground almonds
1 cup dried apricots

Cover the apricots with water or wine in a saucepan and heat until they have plumped up. Mash or blend the butter, gin, sugar and ground almonds in a blender or food processor and serve with the hot apricots.

CABBAGE LEAF PIE

3 Tbsps flour
2 eggs
1/2 cup cream
2 Tbsps sugar
Pinch salt
1/2 tsp cinnamon
1 cooking apple, peeled, cored & sliced
Savoy cabbage leaves, blanched quickly to soften

Flatten the cabbage leaves over the bottom of a high-sided pie dish. Mix together the flour, eggs, cream, sugar, salt and cinnamon. Fold the apple slices into the batter and pour into the cabbage leaf mould. Sprinkle with 1 Tbsp brown sugar and bake in the top of the oven at 425F/220C for 20 minutes. Fold apple into batter. Flatten cabbage leaves over bottom of pie pan, rib side down, pour in batter, sprinkle with 1 Tbsp brown sugar and 1 Tbsp melted butter. Bake in top of oven 20 minutes.

RICE THUNDER & LIGHTNING

2 cups cooked, long-grain rice
2 cups whipped cream
2 Tbsps golden syrup or maple syrup
2 Tbsps raisins

Mix together all the above ingredients and serve.

GRANOLA COOKIES

3/4 cup granola
2 Tbsps raisins
3/4 cup flour
2 Tbsps butter
3 Tbsps sugar
1 egg

Cream the butter and sugar together and beat in the egg. Mix into the granola and add raisins. Put teaspoonfuls onto a greased cookie sheet and bake for 10-15 minutes in a 350F/180C oven.

CHOCOLATE PIZZA

Melt 4 large chunks of chocolate with 1 Tbsp butter in a double boiler or microwave. Stir in 1/2 cup chopped walnuts and spread thinly onto a pizza plate. Freeze. Remove from the freezer, cover with whipped cream and sliced strawberries and gently roll up using a scraper. Serve decorated with more fresh fruit and whipped cream.

WHOLEMEAL TORTE

4 digestive biscuits
Whipped cream
Cream cheese
Grated chocolate
Mint leaves

Put digestive biscuits on a plate and top with whipped cream or cream cheese or both. Sprinkle with grated chocolate and decorate with a fresh mint leaf.

RHUBARB CRUMBLE

Rhubarb, washed and sliced diagonally or 1 packet frozen
3 slices fresh ginger, julienned
2 Tbsps brown sugar
1 Tbsp butter
2 Tbsps porridge oats
1/2 tsp cinnamon

Gently stew the rhubarb with the chopped ginger, sugar and a little water until just tender. Pour into a small baking dish. Mix together the sugar, butter, oats and cinnamon and press on top of the rhubarb. Bake in a 450F/230C oven for 10-15 minutes or until the top is brown and crispy.

PEAR TATIN

2 pears, peeled, halved & cored
1 Tbsp butter
2 Tbsps brown sugar
1/2 package frozen puff pastry, thawed

Melt the butter and sugar in an ovenproof skillet over medium heat. When bubbling, lay in the pear halves. Roll out the puff pastry fairly thin and gently lay over the pears. Trim the edges and bake in a 425F/220C oven for 10-15 minutes. When well browned, remove from the oven, place a plate over the top and flip over onto the plate with the pears showing uppermost. Serve warm.

FRUIT SALAD IN HALF A PINEAPPLE

Slice a pineapple lengthways and hollow out one half. Fill with some blueberries, top with yoghurt and garnish with raspberries and mint leaves.

CROUTES AUX PRUNES (Plums & Fried Bread)

1 can plums or fresh plums
2 thick slices bread
2 Tbsps butter
Whipped cream

Remove the crusts from the bread and fry in the butter until golden brown. Meanwhile heat the plums gently in a saucepan. Arrange the bread on a plate, place the plums on each slice and top with whipped cream (mixed with whatever liqueur you have).

CHOCOLATE SANDWICH

1 box chocolate wafers
Whipped cream

Take a plate and lay a line of whipped cream on the bottom. Take a chocolate wafer and spoon on some cream, add another chocolate wafer and more cream and place on the line of cream on the plate. Gradually build up a chocolate log (drizzle with liqueur if you wish), cover with more whipped cream and freeze. Cut lengthwise to expose the different layers.

STUFFED PEACH HALVES

1 can peach halves or fresh peaches, peeled & halved
1 Tbsp butter
2 Tbsps sugar
2 egg yolks
3/4 cup ground almonds

Cream together the butter, sugar, egg yolks and almonds. Stuff the mixture into the peach halves and bake for 15 minutes in a 400F/200C oven.

ALMOND COTTI

1 cup flour
1/2 cup butter
2 Tbsps icing sugar
7/8 cup/113g ground almonds
1/4 tsp almond extract
Pinch of salt

Cream together all the above ingredients. Form into small balls and bake on an ungreased cookie sheet for 10-15 minutes in a 400F/200C oven. Roll, while still warm, in more icing sugar. Cool. Pile mandarins into a pyramid and arrange the balls amongst them.

GINGERBREAD COOKIES

1/4 cup butter
1 cup brown sugar
1/4 cup molasses
1 egg

Cream all the previous ingredients and then beat in:

2 1/4 cups flour
1 tsp baking soda
1/2 tsp salt
1 tsp ground cinnamon
1 tsp ground cloves or grated nutmeg
1 tsp ground ginger

Form into balls, or cut out shapes with a cookie cutter, sprinkle both sides with granulated sugar and press onto an ungreased cookie sheet. Bake for 15 minutes in a 350F/180C oven.

FRUIT MERINGUE

4 Tbsps mincemeat
2 Tbsps brandy
3 egg whites
1/2 tsp cream of tartar
1 Tbsp white sugar

Mix the mincemeat and brandy together and place in a small, ovenproof dish. Beat the egg whites, cream of tartar and sugar until they stand up softly in peaks. Don't over beat. Pile the meringue on top of the mincemeat and bake for 10 minutes in a 400F/200C oven.

APPLE SLICES

1 apple, thickly sliced
2 Tbsps butter
3 slices ginger, julienned
1/2 tsp sugar
Eggnog

2 Tbsps brandy

Melt the butter in a frypan and add the ginger. Stir well and lay in the apple slices. Gently sauté on each side and pour in 2 Tbsps brandy. Set alight. Pour some eggnog onto a plate and arrange the apple slices on top. Sprinkle with a little sugar, decorate with the ginger and serve.

CHERRIES JUBILEE

1 Tbsp butter
1 Tbsp sugar
1 can cherries - strained
1 orange
2-4 Tbsps Cointreau

Melt the butter with the sugar over a 350 F/180 C heat and stir in the cherries. Squeeze in the orange juice, pour over the Cointreau and set light. Flambé and serve immediately over ice cream..

COCONUT JUMBLES

2 Tbsps butter
2 Tbsps sugar
1 egg, beaten
1 cup flour
1/2 cup grated coconut, unsweetened

Cream the butter and sugar. Stir in the beaten egg and add the flour and coconut. Mix well and form into small balls. Press onto a greased cookie sheet and bake in a 425F/220C oven for 10-12 minutes. Dust with confectioners sugar or finely grated coconut.

DRINKS

WASSAIL CUP

3 red apples
4 cups brown ale
1 cup sherry or white wine
1/2 tsp cinnamon
1/4 tsp grated nutmeg
3-4 slices fresh ginger
2 pieces of lemon peel
Zest of 1/2 lemon and 1/2 orange

Bake the apples either in the oven for 20 minutes or in the microwave for 6 minutes at power 5. Put the rest of the ingredients into a large saucepan and simmer for 5 minutes. Add the apples and serve.

GINGER TEA

2" piece ginger - grated or chopped
4 cups water

4 tsps brown sugar

Juice of a lemon

Bring all the ingredients to a boil and simmer, covered, for about 20 minutes. Strain and drink it hot or leave to cool and keep in the fridge. Dilute with soda water and use for ginger ale. To get more juice from the lemon, put the whole, unpeeled lemon into the tea for about 5-10 minutes then remove and squeeze out the juice.

HOT TODDY

Pour 1 or 2 ozs gin into a glass. Put a spoon in and top up the glass with hot water. Add 1 tsp honey, a cinnamon stick and a slice of lemon and serve hot.

ORANGE JUICE SODA

Blend 1/2 can of frozen orange juice with an equal amount of soda water until frothy. Pour into a glass and decorate with fresh mint leaves and a slice of fresh orange.

CIDER BLACK VELVET

Mix equal portions of cider and Guinness instead of champagne and Guinness.

LASSI

1/2 cup yoghurt

1/2 cup water

Ice-cubes

1/2 tsp salt

1/2 tsp sugar

Blend all the above ingredients together. Pour into a glass and sprinkle with a couple of drops of orange flower water or rose water.

NON-ALCOHOLIC PUNCH

Stir 2 Tbsps sugar into a pot of hot tea. Pour the hot tea onto ice-cubes in a large punch bowl. Dilute with ginger ale and orange juice. Add cucumber slices, orange and lime slices, some grapes and any other fruit you have and float some fresh mint leaves on the top.

CHAMPAGNE PUNCH

Pour 3/4 glass of champagne and top up with orange juice. Add a small shot of Cointreau (or any other orange flavoured liqueur) and garnish with an orange slice and fresh mint leaf.

CRANBERRY APERITIF

3/4 cup soda water

1 8oz/227ml can jellied cranberry sauce

1 tsp sugar

Blend all the above ingredients in a blender and pour into 2 glasses. Add ice and top up with more soda water if necessary. Garnish with lemon slices.

INDEX

INDEX

INDEX

INDEX

INDEX

INDEX

INDEX